Johanna Schuh
Naikan – The World of Introspection. Finding Inner Peace and Discovering Yourself.

Naikan –
The World of Introspection

Finding Inner Peace and Discovering Yourself

Johanna Schuh

Naikan – The World of Introspection
Finding Inner Peace and Discovering Yourself

Johanna Schuh founded the Insightvoice Naikan Centre in Vienna in 2005, which she has since been directing. She started her Naikan practise in 1993 and has been working as a Naikan guide since 2000.

www.insightvoice.at
www.naikan.ws/english

© tao.de in J. Kamphausen Mediengruppe GmbH, Bielefeld

First edition 2016

First published in German under the title *"Naikan – Die Welt der Innenschau"* by tao.de J. Kamphausen in 2014

Author: Johanna Schuh

Translated by K.J.M.

Design & Cover design: Johanna Schuh
Cover photo: Dietmar Meinert / pixelio.de
Cartoon page 3: Johannes & Wolfram

Printed in Germany

Publisher: tao.de in J. Kamphausen Mediengruppe GmbH, Bielefeld, www.tao.de, eMail: info@tao.de

Bibliographic information published by the Deutsche Nationalbibliothek: The Deutsche Nationalbibliothek lists this publication in the Deutsche Nationalbibliografie; detailed bibliographic data are available in the Internet at http://dnb.de.

ISBN: 978-3-95802-970-5 (Paperback)
        978-3-95802-971-2 (Hardcover)
        978-3-95802-972-9 (e-Book)

All rights reserved. No part of this publication may be reproduced, stored in a retrieval system, or transmitted, in any form or by any means without the prior written permission of the publisher, nor be otherwise circulated in any form of binding or cover other than that which it is published and without a similar condition being imposed on the subsequent purchaser.

Contents

Foreword by Setsuko Nakano 9
Foreword by Prof. Akira Ishii 11
Introduction 13

1. Finding inner peace and discovering yourself 17
Classic Naikan: The Naikan week 23
Naikan — long or short? 27

2. Naikan — How does it work? 29
Three questions — a simple tool 35
The 1st Naikan question: What has person X done for me? 41
The 2nd Naikan question: What have I done for person X? 47
The 3rd Naikan question: What difficulties have I caused person X? ... 53
The darn 4th question, which loses it's power 59
Three questions change you 65
The importance of the three questions 69
Lying and stealing 73
Classic Naikan and multi-variant Naikan 77
The Naikan technique and the Naikan depth effect 81
The power of silence 87
Creating order in your inner being 93
Gentle, respectful accompaniment 97
Everything is allowed 103

3. Naikan — How does such a retreat work? 107
Retreat, silence and comfort 111
Organizing your own life story: Biography work 115
The Naikan conversation 119
What are Naikan guides for? 123

The bow 127
Remember, think, empathize 129
The ups and downs of concentration 131
Writing in the book of life 133
Freedom of movement 135
Work meditation 137
The delicious food 139
Can one attend a Naikan retreat more than once? 141

4. Naikan — Can I do this alone in everyday life? 149
Naikan throughout the day — simple and effective 151
Naikan with the focus on a specific person 153
Naikan with the focus on your partner 155
Naikan with the focus on a topic 157
Naikan in the here and now 161
Naikan with the focus on the future 163
Naikan annual review and outlook 165
Naikan biography work 167
Written Naikan 171

5. Naikan — Why should I do it? 173
I want to find peace and recharge my batteries 175
I'm curious — self-awareness 177
I am suffering — self-healing and self-help 179
I am looking — self-realization and spirituality 181
Can anyone practise Naikan? 183

6. Naikan — What does it do for me? 185
Self-realization, self-confidence, self-acceptance 187
Overcoming the past 189
New perspectives and new opportunities 191
Mindfulness and inner peace 193
Living in peace — with myself, everybody and everything 195

7. Naikan — Where does it come from? 197
How Naikan became a method 199
The Buddhist roots 203
The big question of life and death 205

8. Naikan — Can I know even more? 209
Where the 'I' and the 'you' come into contact 211
From either this or that… to both this and that 215
The eternal question of blame 217
The step towards reconciliation 219
The thing called gratitude 221
The past and the here and now 223
Nothing special 225
Freedom 227
Misunderstood Naikan 229
Living Naikan 231

9. Naikan — Where can I attend a retreat? 233
How can I prepare for my Naikan retreat? 235
What I can expect at a Naikan retreat 237
What should I be aware of after the Naikan retreat? 241

Epilogue 243

Footnotes & Literature 247

About the author 253

FOREWORD by Setsuko Nakano

It was in 1997, at the International Naikan Congress in Brixen, Italy, when I met Johanna for the first time. I remember being very moved when I heard a song that touched my heart deeply. It was Johanna's voice. Not only her voice was beautiful, but so was she. At that time she was a Naikan assistant at Naikido, headed by Josef Hartl.

Years later, in 2000, she presented wonderful songs at the International Naikan Congress in Japan. Once again, I was pulled in and fascinated by Johanna's voice. At this congress I heard about Naikan as part of drug treatment, which really impressed me.

After the International Naikan Congress in Germany in 2010, I had the opportunity to visit Johanna's Naikan centre in Vienna. It was a very nice centre. Johanna spontaneously made music with a Japanese Duri player there, and sang to the tunes of the Japanese bamboo instrument. That was very interesting.

After the International Naikan Congress in Japan in 2013, I had the honour of having Johanna practise Naikan at my centre for two weeks. During the Naikan accompaniment of Johanna, who is also a Naikan centre director, my heart was purified. I had an amazing time there. I understood her enthusiasm for Naikan and her sense of music. I think Johanna is a Naikan centre director who will play a leading role for Naikan in Europe.

As a person who also deals with Naikan, I wish that it would spread further through the world and that many people focus on and read this book.

Setsuko Nakano
Head of the Shinshu Naikan Centre, Japan

FOREWORD by Prof. Akira Ishii

Johanna has accompanied many Naikan participants since 1994.

During the time of her Naikan path, Johanna practised Naikan in Europe and in Japan. This book, about the nature of Naikan, was written in clear terms based on this long-standing, deep experience — so that all people can understand it.

This is an important book that can be read both as an introduction to Naikan, as well as to deepen one's already existing Naikan knowledge.

Naikan is a path to happiness, just because of the fact that one sees oneself. I hope that many people come into contact with Naikan through this book and practise Naikan themselves and become happy. It would be nice if you let yourself get inspired through reading, and discover the ability to be happy within yourself.

Prof. Akira Ishii
Professor at Aoyama Gakuin University, Japan

© Photo: Dietmar Meinert / pixelio.de

Introduction

We live in a culture that offers an infinite abundance of external forces. One can very easily lose one's own inner world. I do not mean the desire for what you would like to have or what you wish to be different. I mean the perception of what is. What's going on inside of me? What are my needs? In what direction am I going in my life?

The opinion that a satisfying life is much more than a full bank account and material security has gained more and more followers in recent decades. Whereas in earlier days it was seen as a luxury to take time for yourself, to take breaks or to attend personal development seminars, nowadays it is an accepted fact. Many techniques and methods are now being offered and are accessible to everyone in order to deal with themselves and their own opportunities and goals. But in everyday life, with its enormous demands, there never seems to be enough time to actually take care of oneself. Faster, better, more — that is the motto, both in professional life and in private life. More and more performance is being demanded, regardless of which personal resources are exploited.

Unfortunately, it often takes more than clear signals for us to make a decision about putting ourselves and our actions to the test. Sometimes a physical illness or psychological distress forces us to stop and take a break. Sometimes we are caught in the same old rut for so long that our inner resources get depleted and lead to a burnout.

Don't wait — act now!

This book introduces Naikan to you, a simple method by which you can turn your gaze inwards and find inner peace, on the one hand every day in daily life, and on the other hand as a retreat — one week is ideal.

"Naikan" is a Japanese word meaning "introspection" or "observing the inside". Naikan invites you to turn your gaze inwards, to recognize and better understand yourself.

Normally, our gaze is focused on external things, we look into the world, at the people and things that surround us. We look at what our partner, children, neighbours, and colleagues at work are doing, how they cause us problems, how bad things are at present in the environment and in the world. Rarely do we look at what runs easily or smoothly in our environment and in the world.

Changing one's perspective and looking inside instead of outside is extremely therapeutic, you find yourself again. Taking a break gives one strength. By using the Naikan questions, you recognize your actions and how you deal with yourself and those around you more clearly. This opens up new possibilities for action.

And the best part is: No one else will tell you what is right and what is wrong. Naikan shows you your OWN reality.

Why this book?

For long-term health, it is important to experience tranquillity as valuable and to recognize the care of the inner-being and one's own forces as a natural, healthy part of life. Learn how to consciously experience things — the pleasant and the unpleasant things. Get out of the merry-go-round and into a mindful, more satisfying life.

An excellent and simple method to train these qualities is Naikan — come to rest, find inner clarity and turn your attention onto yourself. Naikan trains the perception of wealth — in the internal and in the external world.

Anyone who asks themselves the three Naikan questions in everyday life, gains more rest, greater clarity and new perspectives in just a few minutes. Anyone who visits a Naikan retreat week gains deep insight into one's own being in just one week.

If this book helps to inspire you to take a step back and pause, then it has served its purpose.

Form and Structure

Each point in each chapter is short and can be read as a self-contained unit. My objective was to present the content in a clear and manageable manner.

As an inspiration, the individual points are accompanied by one image and a thematically appropriate saying. With this I want to encourage you to pause and take a break.

I ask my readers to be understanding with regard to the fact that I have used the masculine and feminine forms wherever applicable, although both genders are meant.

Observations, my own experiences, and Naikan experiences with more than 300 people, who I had the privilege of accompanying, are included in this book. After 20 years of working with this method, I am under the impression that a lot of knowledge, with regard to the theory and practise of Naikan, still has to be tapped into. This life is a fascinating journey of discovery.

From the style of the book you can see that I am an analytical mind, one which likes clarity and wants to know everything exactly. But any theory must be associated with feeling and experience — Naikan has taught me that and has changed my life. Perhaps this is the Naikan message that has impressed me the most: I can stay as I am, and I can acquire additional skills. Or more correctly: I can be myself more and more.

Johanna Schuh
wishes you peace, strength and joy in life.

1. Finding inner peace and discovering yourself

Peace has become very scarce in our culture. Our ears are constantly being flooded with noises: conversations, radio, television, music from headphones, ringing of mobile phones, traffic noises… Also our eyes are constantly being overloaded with images: television, advertising, computers, smartphones, as well as movement in the streets and in shopping malls…

If the outside is so loud and demanding, then it is no surprise that it has become difficult to feel inner peace. People increasingly have the feeling that they have lost touch with themselves. They feel externally driven and can no longer perceive that renowned inner voice.

Naikan's primary message is: It is possible to live in peace and quiet. If you practise turning your attention inwards again and again, then you can find peace — no matter how turbulent the outside is. The Naikan method can be a helpful tool for this.

How do I find inner peace?

This question is becoming increasingly important in our performance-oriented and fast-paced lives. It seems that our culture has forgotten to pause, to take a break. We stumble blindly from one action to the next. We often see the solving of problems as doing more and being even faster.

While the key to problem-solving often lies in retiring and observing the situation calmly. The Naikan method invites you to do exactly that: Retire from your everyday life for a while. Grant yourself a break! Spending a week in silence is ideal for this.

Discovering yourself

It is a modern trend to optimize oneself. The reason for working on oneself is often that the present situation doesn't fit to what is desired. One doesn't want something, one wants to do something about it.

Naikan goes in the other direction. It is about finding a way to deal with everything that is present, and to identify as many aspects and perspectives of life as possible. It is a journey of discovery of one's own being.

Pause for a moment with Naikan

Take a deep breath. Actually, right now.

Direct your focus inwards and be aware of what I would like to show you. Feel it. Simply be aware of what you are feeling, calmness or movement, which impulses emerge, which questions come to mind, which desires arise.

Learn that you do not immediately have to respond to the impressions, impulses and desires. Immediate action is not wanted in these quiet minutes of reflection. Simply try to perceive. Perceive what is, at this moment. That's all.

I have just presented you with a simple exercise for mindfulness.

Naikan adds a simple question technique to this pause:

1st Naikan question:
Who has done something for me? What do I receive?
2nd Naikan question:
What am I doing for the other person? What am I giving?
3rd Naikan question:
What am I doing that creates difficulties?

Perceiving what is, at this moment — and finding clarity with three simple questions. What is currently going on? What comes from the outside? What exactly is my own part? Naikan means pausing and paying attention to oneself.

Is that difficult?

No. The technique is simple. The difficulty here is that we need time and practise to change habits.

Is that possible at the flick of a switch?

At this point you should be warned of a popular misconception: With this is not meant that you will be internally peaceful and calm at the flick of a switch. Unfortunately it doesn't work that easily. Sometimes having a quiet moment makes it clear just how turbulent one's internal being is at that moment.

It's not about changing the current state instantly, but about first perceiving the current state at all. If it is internally turbulent, then it's just turbulent. If you never allow yourself time and rest to pay attention to yourself, then you will not even notice what is going on in your inner life. The corollary of this is that many things occur unconsciously. One feels at the mercy of certain things. Incidentally, this is one of the reasons why some people are a little afraid to take time to rest and retreat: They are not accustomed to paying attention to themselves. If you haven't paid attention to yourself and what is going on inside of you for a long time, then you may think a little fearfully: Who knows what will come up from deep inside?

The answer is simple: It shows what part of you wants attention. And when it finally gets attention, then you can work through it and find a good way to deal with it.

Perceiving. Accepting. Only dealing with it then.

Accept the status quo. Accept it the way it is. It is neither good nor bad, it's just part of you.

We unfortunately skip the first two steps very often in everyday life. We immediately act, we want to change things instantly. And then we wonder why we don't succeed. We have already done soooo much!

We behave like a cook who is seasoning a meal while not perceiving whether it is a vegetable stir-fry or a fruit salad. If we do not perceive what the actual issue is, how can change even occur at all? Chance mainly governs here.

Or we behave like a cook who is seasoning a meal and sees that it is a fruit salad, but doesn't want to accept that, because after all, the vegetable stir-fry was in the fruit salad's place a minute ago. If we do not recognize what the issue is, how can our actions then be appropriate for the situation? How often do we act according to the motto: Now more than ever! Simply because we do not want to accept what our perception has clearly shown.

Inner peace grows when we perceive and accept what is.

Accepting doesn't mean finding everything wonderful and great and forgetting any criticism. Nor does it mean to resign and accept everything passively. Accepting means to look at the facts. That which is, is fine. And at the same time there are things that you can change, and goals that you want to achieve.

Rediscover ancient knowledge

Knowledge about the healing power of peace of body, mind and spirit, has existed for millennia. Every culture, every religion, every path of spiritual training knows methods of retreat and contemplation. Thereby there are always two spheres of activity:

- Methods of regular or daily exercise
- Methods of retreat from everyday life for an extended period

Naikan is a method that can be used both as a tool in everyday life as well as in the form of a time-out.

Naikan is not a religion, although it originated in Japan from the Buddhist worldview. Ishin Yoshimoto, the founder of Naikan, wanted to create a practise of introspection that is accessible and actionable for every person — regardless of his beliefs, regardless of his place in society, regardless of his physical fitness, regardless of his personal opinions.

Naikan neither offers wisdom teachers, nor ideology.

The method is designed for you to find insight from your own experiences. Self-competence and responsibility for oneself are at the forefront.

Drawing from your own knowledge

How often do you ask yourself when you want answers? Can you hear the answers that are coming from within? How do you deal with what you know and feel inside?

We prefer asking other people when we are seeking answers. But can someone else really tell you what the right path is for you personally? If we always look for answers on the outside, then that is a constant source of unrest. Ultimately only the answers that come from ourselves help. Naikan trains the ability to have an internal dialogue with oneself.

If you listen to yourself in order to get answers to your questions, you often receive quite contradictory signals from inside. Perhaps you react in a disappointed manner or have an internal quarrel with yourself. This is also a source of unrest. The healthy way to deal with inconsistencies is by perceiving them, and including these in your decision.[1] Naikan trains the ability to deal with the sometimes conflicting diversity of experiences, and to find clarity.

The tower of strength

Rest and movement are a constant interplay. This is true for the inner workings, as well as for the world that surrounds us. To deal with this moving interplay, we yearn for peace and quiet, for a tower of strength.

We like to look for support and orientation from the outside. But we won't find anything there. Finally, we see that it is about internal support and orientation.

Again and again people come to Naikan to find their own centre, their calming anchor. One participant also came with this request, and recognized the following on the sixth day of her Naikan-week: "I can be my own tower of strength."

Welcome to the world of introspection.

Classic Naikan: The Naikan week

When the Naikan method came to Europe in the 1980s, it was clear for a long time that "Naikan" meant a retreat week. Over time, the diversity of Naikan forms grew, which is very pleasing.

Today, however, it is no longer clear when one speaks of Naikan and says: "I have done Naikan," whether it was for a week, a weekend or a quick getting-to-know the method at a seminar. Was it Classic Naikan, Kodo Naikan, Naikan coaching? Was it solely Naikan, or Naikan in combination with another method?

In order to create a disambiguation, the 'Association of Classic Naikan' was founded in 2010 in Austria. The objective of the association is to represent, maintain, and clearly display the Classic Naikan week to the outside world.

What is Classic Naikan?

The definition of "Classic Naikan", in terms of the Association of Classic Naikan, quoted on http://www.naikan-verband.net:

Naikan introspection allows the growths of one's self-awareness and personal development in a holistic manner. Introspection and self-knowledge are the basis for the recognition, understanding, comprehension, experience, development, and the acceptance of one's own nature in all areas of human existence — on a spiritual, mental, emotional and physical level.

Classic Naikan is a one week retreat in silence and introspection. Methodological tools are the 3 Naikan questions:

1st Naikan question: What has [Person X] done for me?
2nd Naikan question: What have I done for [Person X]?
3rd Naikan question: What difficulties have I caused [Person X]?

The Naikan participants are accompanied by a trained Naikan guide or a team of Naikan guides during the Naikan week. The Naikan accompaniment is carried out in individual sessions (no group work).

Conditions:

• Duration of a Naikan week: A minimum of 6 whole exercise days (continuously from dawn to dusk), including 7 nights (e.g. Sunday evening to Sunday morning).

• Structure of the day: A minimum of 14 hours of Naikan exercise per day from the start of the day (waking up) until the end of the day (going to sleep).

• Structure of the week: At the beginning of the week the Naikan guide gives the Naikan participants an introduction (organizational as well as content-related information). After the introduction: The beginning of the Naikan exercise, retreat to the place of practise and thereafter silence until the end of the Naikan exercise. Self-reflection is supported through individual private Naikan conversations with the Naikan guide. On the last day the Naikan guide ensures a good completion of the Naikan week in the sense that the participant is well prepared for everyday life.

• Each Naikan participant receives a private training area for the individual self-reflection during the Naikan week. This is to retreat and focus on yourself.

• From the beginning of the Naikan exercise on the first day up until the last day, continuous silence between Naikan participants and no contact to the outside world is agreed on (no conversing and making contact, no phones, no computers), also no distractions are allowed (no television, no radio, no reading). Contact during the Naikan week is solely with Naikan guides.

• The Naikan guides come to the Naikan participants several times a day to lead individual Naikan conversations. During the course of the day, there are at least 7 individual meetings at intervals of 60 to 120 minutes.

• Naikan is understood as a continuous practise, without interruption (e.g. silence also during meals), and in autonomous self-reflection (i.e. most of the work is done by the Naikan participants themselves, at their own pace at their place of practise, without interference from external sources).

• The Naikan exercise works with the 3 Naikan questions:

1st Naikan question: What has [.........] done for me?
2nd Naikan question: What have I done for [.........]?
3rd Naikan question: What difficulties have I caused [.........]?

• First of all, the Naikan questions are asked with regard to people (e.g. mother, father, grandparents, siblings, partners…). The memories in relation to a person are chronologically examined using the 3 Naikan questions, from the first contact until today, or until the last contact. This is divided into stages of life (about 4 to 6 years). For every stage of life, there is 60 to 120 minutes of reflection time for the Naikan participants, who find a certain closure through a short individual Naikan conversation with a Naikan guide. (Example: Person — mother, when I was 0-6 years old, then 6-10, 10-14, 14-18, etc. until today)

• Individual Naikan meetings are usually short (about 10 minutes). Here, the Naikan participant reports about some of the examples that he or she has found regarding the 3 Naikan questions. The Naikan guide listens attentively and thanks the participant. Support through genuine listening, restraint and being non-judgmental are the main tasks of Naikan guides. If the Naikan participant has questions or concerns, he or she can discuss these with the Naikan guide. If necessary, the Naikan guide is there to give additional guidance.

• The core of the Naikan method is to work with the 3 Naikan questions. Normally, it does not need additional methodological supplements. If necessary, the Naikan guide can support the participant with other tools.

• As a rule, the Naikan exercise begins with the observation of one's own life story in relation to the mother (or the person who has taken on the mother role), then in relation to the father. Subsequently, it is individually agreed upon which persons or topics will be dealt with using the Naikan questions.

Naikan — long or short?

How much time should you spend on self-reflection? Does Naikan always have to be for a week? What's the point of only doing Naikan for one or two days? And are introspection and inner peace possible in everyday life?

To avoid any misunderstanding: Yes, the ideal time for Naikan is a whole week.

Why? It takes two to three days until you really get used to the environment and the calmness and can leave your worries behind. Then it takes a further two days until your inner peace is so stable that deeper inner regions of the self can be perceived. And from the fifth or sixth day, you will become more and more successful at just perceiving what your inner being is showing you. Problems and solutions fade into the background. Core issues slowly become visible and conscious.

It is also possible to continuously practise Naikan for several weeks. Going into depth in complete peace — the meditative character of Naikan fully develops with a prolonged retreat.

The duration of the silence and exercise decides how deeply you can introspect.

But are short forms so bad?

I say no. Many Naikan participants taught me that even Naikan days can be very well used. Even if you have never done Naikan. What matters is the motivation. He or she, who really wants to deal with themselves with regard to a particular person (or a specific topic), can benefit from the peace and the Naikan questions on one or two days as well.

You must just want it, as the saying goes. This also applies to the integration of introspection and peace in everyday life. It is possible!

*To know thyself
is the beginning of wisdom.*

Socrates

2. Naikan – How does it work?

Naikan comes from Japan and is a method of introspection to explore one's own self. The Japanese word "Naikan" translates into inner observation or introspection.

 "Nai"= inside, the interior

 "kan"= observing, looking, looking out for

It is about really seeing oneself, about deeply recognizing one's own being, and about meditative self-reflection. No, it's not an ego trip, because you look at your own behaviour with regard to other people — exactly where the 'I' and the 'you' meet.

The Naikan method works with three simple questions that can be used at any time — in ordinary everyday life.

> The three Naikan questions:
> 1. What has the person, who I am taking into account, done for me?
> 2. What have I done for this person?
> 3. What difficulties have I caused this person?

By looking at these three questions, you can focus on the constructive areas in contact with others. A well-known, but rarely useful question, loses power:

4. What difficulties has this person caused me?

No evaluation, no judgement.
Just see what actually is.
That's Naikan.

And off you go!

- Select a person (e.g. mother, father, son, daughter, partner, friend, boss, co-worker…)
- Define a specific time period (e.g. today, last week, last year, the months from — to, the years from — to…)
- Remember things that you experienced in this period, explore your memories about the experiences with that person, in that period.
- Then ask the three Naikan questions.

Have you already tried it?

No? Then it would be best to read the previous lines once again, and then take three minutes to try Naikan in practise. You know it: You can only know how an apple tastes, if you have bitten into it yourself. You have to experience it yourself, it is not enough to read about it.

You've tried Naikan now? Then you have probably noticed that the Naikan method works very easily. You can practise it immediately and at any time.

Is it really that simple?

Yes. The Naikan technique works in a very simple manner. The difficult part is to actually start the exercise.

With each new task that we have in mind, we must first start — and unfortunately, it often doesn't go much further than a good intention. Therefore, it is favourable if you begin with a Naikan retreat week.

If you practise Naikan at a retreat, then you will be accompanied in your introspection by experienced Naikan guides. As a Naikan participant, you yourself explore your life and find insights. Your own experiences count.

Naikan guides listen attentively, with deep respect and great appreciation for every single person.

What now — the everyday technique or a retreat?

Naikan can be both an in-depth self-exploration in the form of a retreat — ideal is one week of Naikan — as well as a simple tool in everyday life.

As a tool in everyday life, you can practise introspection and, with the help of the Naikan questions, bring clarity into your actions.

In a Naikan retreat you have the opportunity to explore your own life story, to arrange it, and, with the three Naikan questions, discover new perspectives and your inner glow.

Three elements are combined in a Naikan seminar:
- The power of silence
- Create order in your emotional life
- Gentle, respectful accompaniment

The power of silence

One consciously rests in a meditative environment. A Naikan seminar is about withdrawing from a noisy and hectic life into silence.

Finally, undisturbed time for yourself.

The silence allows deep inner layers to become perceptible again. The inner dialogue, which is too often neglected in everyday life, becomes active again. The inner voice can be heard and perceived again.

In this sense, Naikan is an intense training for perception and mindfulness.

Create order in your emotional life

This protected environment allows you to explore your own life and to rediscover your own memories. What makes you the person you are today, is what you have experienced. What you do today is nourished by what you have experienced in the past. Three questions bring order into your own past and allow you to clearly recognize the possibilities for action in the present and the future. A colourful and clear picture arises of how you have created your "life story" up to now, and how it will continue.

You explore your own life and structure the events which you can remember:

- Place a certain person in the centre of observation (first mother, then father, siblings, partner…). A certain topic (e.g. career, health…) can later be tested using the Naikan method.

- You have a clearly limited time period involved and continue to follow your own life (e.g. when you were 0-6 years old, then 6-10, then 10-14 years etc. to this day).

- Your memories shine through with the help of three Naikan questions.

In this sense, Naikan is structured and comprehensive biographical work.

Gentle, respectful accompaniment

During a Naikan week you will be individually and respectfully supported and accompanied by experienced Naikan guides. Naikan guides listen attentively, do not judge, and approach each person individually. Everything, which appears, is allowed.

Firstly, Naikan guides ensure conditions conducive to the practise of Naikan taking place in an undisturbed and secure environment: design of the Naikan space, structuring of the daily routine, supplying of meals, among other things. The Naikan guides are there for you around the clock during your Naikan seminar.

Secondly — and this is essential — Naikan guides accompany you through the internal processes that arise during the practise of Naikan. Each person is unique, so internal experiences are very individual. The Naikan accompaniment therefore requires care and sensitivity. The Naikan guides will have private conversations with each person approximately eight to ten times a day.

Can everyone practise Naikan?

Naikan is suitable for people of all ages. The only requirement for the practise of Naikan is the ability to differentiate memory and reality from fantasy and fiction.

People come to Naikan who…

- are just curious and want to get to know themselves better
- have current difficulties (e.g. relationship crisis, problems at work, decision problems, burnout issues, etc.)
- want to deal with a problem (e.g., illness, addiction, etc.)
- face questions of being, who want to realize spirituality.

Naikan is the wrong thing for you if you are looking for a doctrine of salvation or a master who will tell you what to do. Because Naikan is a simple method that supports you in your self-actualization.

Naikan is right for you if you want to experience the power of silence and learn an easy way for your self-exploration.

And what is this for?

Everyone who has practised Naikan in a retreat feels richer, more relaxed, and more peaceful. They are surprised and filled with joy because they have discovered positive experiences again. Some problems have lost power in their lives. A Naikan participant wrote the following to me: "I feel a certain warmth, a fulfilment, and above all a relief in my being."

The goal of Naikan is to consciously perceive everything that surrounds us. A Naikan participant said to me: "Naikan makes me complete." It is about perceiving ourselves and the world how we really are, and not how we want to see them, or should see them. It may not always be pleasant to perceive yourself this way and to observe yourself on diverse levels, but that makes us complete and allows us to live in peace, here and now.

*If you want
a wise answer,
ask a reasonable question.*

Johann Wolfgang von Goethe

Three questions — a simple tool

The core of the Naikan method is the technique of asking three questions.

> The three Naikan questions:
> 1. What has the person, who I am taking into account, done for me?
> 2. What have I done for this person?
> 3. What difficulties have I caused this person?

The Naikan questions allow you to learn to see the facts clearly, and not to mix them up with feelings, judgements and so on. You clearly recognize your own part in what you have experienced. This puts your potentials and possibilities in focus; The more clearly you perceive these, the better you can alter outdated or inappropriate action and thought patterns, and lead a fulfilled life.

In all experiences and interactions that one has, there are parts or contributions which come from the other individual, and parts which emanate from yourself. Naikan shows this in a simple way: The 1st Naikan question shows the other person's contribution, the 2nd and the 3rd Naikan questions explore your own part.

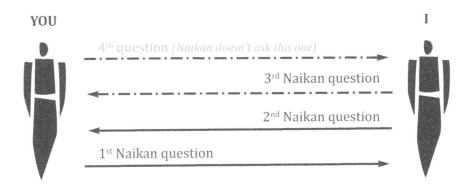

We usually think of experiences as a complete package. That's actually a good thing, because we aren't able to constantly consider all the details. Sometimes, however, the details need to be looked at so that we can deal with situations differently.

With the Naikan questions you can separate the following:

What was the other person's part? In Naikan language: What has this person done for me?

What was my own contribution or part? In Naikan language: What have I done for this person? What difficulties have I caused this person?

See facts

Moreover, Naikan encourages you to see the facts clearly. It's about learning to recognize actions and not to mix them up with emotions, thoughts, and expectations, which may have come up parallel during another action.[2]

Suppose you are concerning yourself with the 1st Naikan question: What has your mother done for you? If your mother baked you a cake for your birthday, then that is something that your mother did. This is a fact, regardless of whether you enjoyed the cake or not, regardless of whether you expected a different cake, regardless of whether you felt feelings of anger or gratitude about it, and regardless of what thoughts you had.

Or an example in your professional life: What has your colleague done for you? One answer might be: He offered you a cup of coffee. That is a fact, regardless of whether you enjoyed the coffee or not, regardless of whether you may have had the impression that he wanted to ingratiate him or herself, regardless of whether the coffee was made especially for you or there was just a cup left over, regardless of whether you were angry with the colleague at the time… The fact is, the colleague offered you a cup of coffee. Period.

Naikan, as a technique for answering questions, brings clarity to one's perception. In this sense, one can see Naikan as perception training.

Collect facts

How do you approach the Naikan questions in practise?

One possibility is to collect matching things to the Naikan questions. I like to compare it to how one would collect berries or mushrooms, or how one would choose flowers for a bouquet.

Think about what you have experienced with a particular person and assign these experiences to the Naikan questions. 1st Naikan question: What has X done for me? For example, X invited me to eat, gave me a gift for my birthday, baked a birthday cake for me, listened to me, gave me some advice one a problem, called me and asked how I was doing… 2nd Naikan question: What have I done for X? For example, I sent X information via e-mail because I know that he or she is interested in said info, I listened to him/her, offered him/her coffee and cake, invited him/her to a concert, brought a souvenir from vacation, called him/her, visited him/her… 3rd Naikan question: What difficulties have I caused person X? For example, I forgot to call X even though it was firmly agreed upon, gave some advice which insulted X, overreacted and hurt X by doing so, didn't listen, didn't make time for them, had a fight…

A nice comparison for Naikan is the way in which we arrange a colourful mess of puzzle pieces or mosaic tiles. A picture emerges gradually — namely the picture of one's own life. From a messy puzzle in one's head and heart, piece by piece, an image emerges which shows one's own path in life.

Analyse facts

Another way to use the Naikan questions, would be to apply all three questions to a particular situation. I take a particular experience that I have had with a person and make the different parts and aspects visible to me using the Naikan questions. This approach is particularly well-suited for you to see your part in a specific situation.

Consider the above-mentioned scenario again — the mother who baked a birthday cake. 1st Naikan question: What has my mother done for me in this situation? For example, she took the time to bake a cake for me, she shopped for all the ingredients, she remembered my birthday and wanted to do something nice for me... 2nd Naikan question: What have I done for my mother in this situation? For example, I thanked her for the cake, ate a piece of it, spent time with my mother, declined another invitation in order to be with my mother... 3rd Naikan question: What difficulties did I cause my mother in this situation? For example, I complained that there was no whipped cream, didn't want to take home the remaining cake, came late, didn't really listen to her...

How do I find facts?

Think about what you have experienced with this person. You can take Naikan in many different directions, such as:

- Material things (gifts, food, clothing, utensils, money, education, work, hobbies...)
- Dialogues (conversations, letters, phone calls, e-mails...)
- Emotional things (trust, support, recognition, appreciation, joy, anger, rage, sadness, pain...)
- Intangible things (knowledge, skills, expertise, experience...)
- Direct contact (things said or given first-hand...)
- Indirect contact (things said or given third-hand, strengthening or damaging someone's reputation...)
- Experiences regarding time (timing, punctuality, time available...)
- Experiences in terms of space (at home and abroad, the choice of the area for encounters, atmosphere, taking in the space, making space available...)
- In connection with living, working, learning, leisure, traveling...
- Things that you classify as (very) important (special occasions, celebrations, sustainable and effective experiences, defining moments...)
- Everyday things (taking things for granted, trivialities, things that you have to do every day...)
- Experiences regardless of whether they were pleasant or unpleasant for you (i.e. regardless of your feelings)
- Experiences regardless of whether they met your expectations and desires or not (i.e. regardless of your judgment)
- ...there is so much to still discover!

Apply the three Naikan questions to the situations which you remember. Remembering alone is not enough, only the Naikan questions allow you to gain a new perspective.

Inner Dialogue

Naikan directs our attention inward, as the name "introspection" implies. I do not ask someone else, but I ask myself about my own behaviour. This is how an inner dialogue takes place.

The willingness to find out what one has contributed to the situation arises. This in turn draws attention to those areas that you can change yourself.

It may sound paradoxical, but although Naikan focuses on facts, the answers to the Naikan questions don't just come from the mind. But rather from a feeling: Let your heart speak. Because your inner voice is speaking in the language of feelings in your inner dialogue.

In other words: An answer to a Naikan question is not only logically correct, but it feels right too.

Since Naikan is based on the internal dialogue, it is a tool that makes you independent. No expert can tell you what you should find in Naikan. As you are the expert in your own life.

If you want to do yourself a favour, then think of the merits of your fellow human beings.

Marcus Aurelius

© Photo: Rainer Sturm / pixelio.de

The 1ˢᵗ Naikan question: What has person X done for me?

1ˢᵗ Naikan question: **What has person X done for me? What have I received?**	2ⁿᵈ Naikan question: **What have I done for this person? What have I given?**
4ᵗʰ question (Naikan doesn't ask this one): What difficulties has this person caused me?	3ʳᵈ Naikan question: **What difficulties have I caused this person?**

The 1ˢᵗ Naikan question is: What has person X done for me?

This question directs our attention to the abundance of things that are done for us every day. Don't only look for special gifts, but just look at what that person has done for you.

Concretely

Always think of concrete situations. Because Naikan is based on facts. What actually happened?

A practical example: You are practising Naikan with your focus being on your partner — time period is the previous year. The following answer is not really significant: "He was always there for me." What does that

41

actually mean? Was he open to having a conversation when it was important to you? Was he at home often when you were also there? Did he stand by you in difficult situations, and how did he do that? Think about what the words "always" and "there for me" mean to you personally. How did your partner behave, what did he say or do for you to be able to say: "He was always there for me"?

Another practical example: You are practising Naikan with your focus being on your mother in childhood, in primary school, when you were between the ages of 6 and 10. The following answer is not really significant: "My mother always cooked." What does that mean — always? Does that mean breakfast, lunch and dinner, or just once a day? Does that mean every day, without exception? What did you eat?

Were the meals a meeting place for the whole family? Was there a specific meal on special occasions? Did she prepare a sandwich for school or give you a piece of fruit? Think about concrete situations, give details. For example, my mother cooked lunch. She often cooked spinach (= 1st Naikan question) and I ate it (= 2nd Naikan question), even though I didn't really like it and threw a fit sometimes, which really annoyed her (= 3rd Naikan question).

It is not enough to make general statements. Try to recall events and situations. What exactly did the other person do for you in that situation? In this sense, Naikan trains your eye for detail.

Not good, not bad — just facts

The 1st Naikan question is: What has person X done for me? The question is not: What good things has person X done for me?

It is probably one of the biggest challenges to see through your own perception of "good" and "bad". It is therefore important to pay attention to how the Naikan questions are formulated. Naikan supports a value-free perspective. It is about looking past what is "good" and "bad", and rather looking at what is actually going on, the fact.

A practical example: You are practising Naikan with your focus being on your work colleague, with whom you had an unpleasant dispute. If you ask: What good things has he done for me? Then you might come up with the fact that he apologized to you after the fight. If you ask: What has he done for me? You may see that he said an inconvenient truth to your face with his allegations — as uncomfortable as it was for you, as inappropriately as he perhaps expressed it, as hurtfully as he behaved, the fact remains that he told you the truth. Would you also find such an answer if you were only looking for the good things?

If, from the get-go, you are only asking what good the other person has done, then you are automatically excluding many experiences and insights. The Naikan recommendation is: Expand your horizons!

The motive

At some point you start to ask yourself: What was the motive? Did this person really do something for me altruistically?

It is wonderful if such details awaken your spirit of inquiry. But please do not get lost in these thoughts. Because no matter how much you seek to find clarity, the true motive of another human being will always remain a mystery to you.

It is more important to determine whether this person has done something for you, and what it was. It is not paramount to know for what reason someone did something.

Some practical examples: Your colleague invited all the employees from the department to celebrate his birthday. Maybe he only invited you because it was the courteous thing to do, and would rather not have you there. The fact is: He also invited you. Your mother cooked for the whole family. She would have cooked anyway, regardless of whether you were there or not. The fact is: You got something to eat, so your mother also cooked for you. Your big sister only took you with on a trip because she was not allowed to go alone. Maybe she didn't really want you to go with. The fact is: You went on the trip.

Yes, but...

It is always amazing to observe how difficult it is for us to change our thought patterns and to just give simple answers to the Naikan questions — without ifs and buts. We love to add justifications, excuses and accusations.

Some practical examples: "Yes, okay, my mother cooked for me — but she forced me to eat everything on my plate. I am still suffering from that today." And then comes the accusation. In Naikan we call it the 4th question. "Yes, okay, my partner accompanied me to the concert but then she constantly criticized everything and spoiled my evening." — "Yes, okay, my colleague took the work off my hands, but she omitted a step and I subsequently had to do twice as much work to fix it!"

We criticize the other person much too often. We have become very comfortable in our attitude of: I am suffering and it's your fault.

Naikan doesn't play this game. Just answer the three questions, period. It is important to identify where your own expectations, estimates, feelings, prejudices, accusations, suspicions and so, disguise, distort or superimpose the facts. In this sense, Naikan has a clarifying effect.

Nothing special

We often try to find very special situations, things that you have experienced as a special gift, something that stands out from daily life. One recalls the birthday gift one fervently wished for and actually got, the school play at which you received special praise, the great holiday, the pay increase…

Yes, these things also count.

Much more productive are the countless little things that are done for us every day — despite or precisely because they are nothing special. What would a day be without a "Hello", a "How was your day?" or a "Good morning"? What would a day be without breakfast, lunch, dinner, and the countless movements that need to be done in preparing the meal? What would a day be without a roof over your head?

Someone ensures that our primary needs regarding food, housing and care are met every day.

This secure base of countless little things makes it possible for us to look forward to something special.

From a shortage to an abundance

Many people live in a sense of having a shortage, and are of the opinion that they received too little.

Constant accusations often accompany us, such as: my mother was at home too little, my father was too strict, I fought with my siblings so much, my teachers were unfair, my boss is an ignoramus, my colleagues don't do their work, my partner doesn't take me into account enough, my relatives only want money…

The list of accusations against the people that surround us are endless. Above all, it shows that the focus is on what you did not get or what was wrong, in your own subjective opinion.

The 1st Naikan question asks you to look at what you received. Often many things come back into focus that this person has done for you.

Perhaps your mother was at home less than you would have liked, but yet she still ensured that you had food, that the laundry was done, that clothes and toys were bought, maybe she cared for you when you were sick, read stories to you… Maybe your partner actually does take you into consideration too little, but yet he or she still gave you gifts, spent time with you, listened to you when you needed a sympathetic ear…

So many things are there, you just need to look at them.

*Only someone
who knows the pleasure of giving,
knows the art of receiving.*

Marie von Ebner-Eschenbach

The 2ⁿᵈ Naikan question: What have I done for person X?

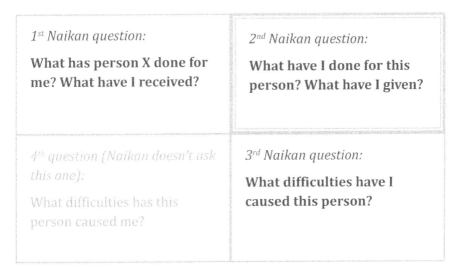

The 2ⁿᵈ Naikan question is: What have I done for person X?

This question directs your attention to what you have done for other people. Yes, you are a person who is able to give. It is worthwhile exploring how your 'doing' and 'being' affected others.

Stay with the facts and include small things and special gifts when answering this question.

Giving is the most natural thing in the world

Often we do not notice what we do for other people, because it is so natural and normal to give. All the more reason to train the eye to see what we do for others. It's good to know your own prospects.

Practising Naikan we often experience that we can remember a lot of things to answer the 1ˢᵗ Naikan question, i.e. what the other person has done for us. However, we find relatively few examples for the 2ⁿᵈ Naikan question.

We are under the impression that we have done a lot less for the other person than they have done for us.

Why is that?

Of course it may be that we have actually done very little for the other person. If this is the case, then it is important to also recognize it.

A mother or a caregiver will always do more for her child than the child will do for her. That is the nature of this role allocation; A helpless baby must first discover the world step by step and learn how to move in it.

More often than not, the apparent imbalance in the give and take lies in a simple truth: Perception is subjective.

As a Naikan guide I have the privilege of meeting many different people and seeing how they perceive the world. I have heard the statements of Naikan participants, who are focusing on their mothers or fathers — they say: "I've done so little for my parents." I have heard the statements of mothers and fathers who say: "The birth of my child was the greatest gift in my entire life, it cannot be described in words." So, who has now done more or less for the other? The parents or the children?

There is no clear answer because it is impossible to measure a subjective experience with regard to give and take.

Nothing should be taken for granted

Over and over I experience people who attach little importance to the 2ⁿᵈ Naikan question. I find that very sad because it is part of being a healthy human, that you are able to see yourself as someone who can give mankind and the world something back — by your own actions, or simply by being you.

A Naikan participant got to the heart of it when she asked, during our Naikan conversation, rather desperately: "What am I doing wrong if I can't think of anything to answer the 2nd Naikan question?" I said: "You think too complicatedly." This woman was the mother of two amazing children, who appreciated her contact and advice, even in adulthood. As she was practising Naikan with the focus on one of her two children, she could not find anything to answer the 2nd Naikan question.

When I asked her if she cooked for her children, did the laundry, helped them with their homework, she exclaimed: "But that's normal!"

Yes, that's true, from our own perspective many things are simply taken for granted and seen as 'normal'.

That's a beautiful thing. Of course, one does not praise oneself for every article of clothing that one has folded, and says: "I am such a gift to humanity!" That would be an ego trip, whereby no one really feels comfortable. Yet it is still important to be aware of what you do for others. As that is how one experiences oneself as a person who can give.

Self-praise doesn't stink

There are people who have difficulties with the 2nd Naikan question because they secretly condemn any form of recognition of one's own actions as self-praise.

We all know the phrase "self-praise stinks!" That's true — but not always.

If self-praise serves to impress, to manipulate, to brag or exaggerate your own performance, then it really does stink. However, there is nothing wrong with proper recognition of what one has done or achieved. This is a very healthy form of self-praise, which is important for our self-image.

It doesn't have to be good

The 2nd Naikan question is: What have I done for person X? The question is not: What good things have I done for person X?

We have a strong tendency to put everything in the category of either "good" or "bad". The formulation of the Naikan questions is deliberately

49

kept neutral so that as many facets as possible, of your own actions, can be shown. Therefore, make sure that you are not limiting your answers to the 2nd Naikan question to the 'good' things.

A practical example: You are practising Naikan with the focus being on a friend. If you ask: What good have I done for him? Then you might remember that you invited him to dinner, gave him a present, listened to him about his heartbreak for hours… If you ask: What have I done for him? Then things come up, which do not necessarily fit into the category of "good", because they were, for example, uncomfortable for the other person.

Perhaps you dragged that friend into a restaurant even though he had no desire to go there, simply because you thought he would get over his heartache by keeping busy. Maybe it was a nice evening, maybe not. Regardless of how the evening went, the fact remains: You dragged him into a restaurant and hoped to help him thereby.

Good intentions

If you practise Naikan, then you will quickly realize that "good intentions" don't automatically go down well with the other person. Yes, it is part of the 2nd Naikan question, that you have done something for the other person because you had good intentions. But please also check how your 'doing' actually comes across. On closer inspection, can you still say that you did it for the other person?

Or have you also caused him difficulties at the same time?

In the aforementioned practical example, you wanted to support your friend by visiting a restaurant. Maybe he enjoyed it. Or maybe you had a dispute because of it, in which case you caused him some difficulties. Both are a possibility.

Wholeheartedly

What we do for others doesn't necessarily have to be done wholeheartedly. The 2nd Naikan question doesn't only entail what we have given someone gladly or willingly. In the practise of Naikan we also include things that you've done accidentally, unconsciously, unintentionally or incidentally for the other person.

Some practical examples: You invited all the colleagues from the department to your birthday party, including Miss N, who you do not really like. The fact is: You also invited Miss N. You cooked for the whole family. The fact is that your daughter got something to eat, so you also cooked for your daughter. You took your little sister with on a trip because you were not allowed to go alone. The fact is: Your sister could join the trip.

Do these examples seem familiar?

Correct! You read these exact examples in the previous chapter, from the other perspective, when answering the 1st Naikan question. There it pointed out that the motive of the other person is irrelevant.

The motive plays a bigger role for your own actions. Because unlike the motives of others, you can actually clarify your own motives. You also shouldn't lose yourself in a causal investigation when answering the 2nd Naikan question, but it is useful to recognize your own motives.

Because if you can see what drives you, then you will not be driven unconsciously. You have more room to manoeuvre when your own motives become clear.

From powerlessness to having the ability to act

We often have the feeling of not being able to do anything. We feel powerless and don't know what we can change. The 2nd Naikan question shows what actions we have set into motion and what contributions we have made to a relationship or a situation. On the basis of this question, we see more clearly what we can do or change from now on.

*Truths which one has trouble hearing,
are the ones
that are particularly necessary.*

Jean de La Bruyère

© Photo: Rainer Sturm / pixelio.de

The 3rd Naikan question: What difficulties have I caused person X?

1st Naikan question: **What has person X done for me? What have I received?**	2nd Naikan question: **What have I done for this person? What have I given?**
4th question (Naikan doesn't ask this one): *What difficulties has this person caused me?*	3rd Naikan question: **What difficulties have I caused this person?**

The 3rd Naikan question is: What difficulties have I caused person X?

This question makes you aware of turbulences and disturbances which you may have caused in coexistence. Where were you a trigger for someone else to have worries, added work, or difficulties? Where have you caused problems? What did you do that the other person struggled to deal with?

Apart from good and evil

Many people find it difficult to face the 3rd Naikan question: What difficulties have I caused? When answering this question one immediately thinks: Where did I do something bad? Where was I a bad person? Negative feelings come alive. But that's not what it is about. Labels like "good" and "evil" do not help.

The 3rd Naikan question is not: Where was I a bad person to person X? It only asks: What difficulties have I caused?

We can cause difficulties intentionally, but more often we do it unintentionally. I cause difficulties, for example, if someone had to do more work because of me, worried about me, was disturbed during his or her activities, was hit on a sensitive spot…

I can also cause difficulties simply by being different from the other person and thus, for example, having different desires, different needs, different timing, different interests… Sometimes this results in conflicts, sometimes you find a good way to deal with it.

For some difficulties, which we have caused, we want to apologize because we are sorry. And there are difficulties, which are as they are, and we are not sorry. Both are fine.

The question of guilt

One of the trickiest aspects of Naikan is the question of guilt. The following concern is often voiced: If I ask the 3rd Naikan question, won't that produce feelings of guilt?

No, Naikan doesn't cause feelings of guilt. On the contrary, it even allows you to say goodbye to guilt feelings. Because having feelings of guilt means that one still wishes it would have been different. To admit guilt, however, means seeing one's own part or contribution clearly, and accepting it.[3]

It's actually quite simple: Either I did something and I take responsibility for it, or not. Yes, every individual has done something which has had negative effects. Sometimes our motive was to harm others, sometimes we just didn't know better. It is important to recognize your own contribution with the 3rd Naikan question. Where have I caused difficulties? What do I have to take responsibility for? What am I guilty of?

If you take responsibility for something that you actually caused, then that is unpleasant and often painful, but at the same time infinitely relieving. It cannot be changed, it happened. You can only take responsibility with an honest and upright approach.

The point of Naikan is not for you to go into an emotional spiral of guilt and self-blame. The 3rd Naikan question simply encourages you to look more closely at your own uncomfortable aspects. Self-condemnation and guilt are intense topics in general, so, as a Naikan guide, I stay clear of negative spirals and support one's inner peace as much as possible.

Lose feelings of guilt

I have experienced several times that people felt free of guilt, because they intensively examined the 3rd Naikan question with regard to a specific matter, and didn't find anything.

This is especially true for guilt that stems from childhood. There was a Naikan participant who practised Naikan with the focus being on her mother. Her mother was depressed and had been this way since the Naikan participant had been a little girl. As children often do, she somehow felt guilty that her mother repeatedly had depressive phases. She was able to see, through Naikan, that her mother's state had not been caused by her as a daughter. This fact made her feel relieved, so the guilt she felt dissipated.

Careful observation is very helpful in Naikan, so that you do not take responsibility for something you did not cause.

I had an eye-opening experience, in this context, with my colleague Ingrid Stempel. She was guiding a Naikan week with several participants. I had taken over the kitchen. One morning, when we were bringing breakfast to the participants, we mixed up the trays with the drinks.

We didn't take it too seriously, and after some back and forth, each participant had their desired drink. Later, Ingrid and I talked about the situation and, as experienced Naikan practitioners, found ourselves being able to see and admit our own mistakes (great!), but also wanting to take responsibility for the whole mess (not great at all!). It became clear as daylight that it was too much of a good thing. I realized that it's about taking responsibility for your own part and not about being the scapegoat for everything.

Of course you have caused difficulties

It is perfectly normal that we cause difficulties, that something doesn't come across well, that we cause turmoil in our environment or in other peoples' lives, that something goes wrong in communication, or that some things don't run smoothly.

A Naikan participant, who is a trainer and coach by profession, asked me, as he was practising Naikan with the focus on his career: "You don't mean to say that I have caused my coaching clients difficulties because I asked them uncomfortable or unexpected questions?" My answer was: "Yes, of course you have caused them difficulties thereby. It may be uncomfortable and not always easy to take." In this case, it was even part of the method, part of the job, to create difficulties.

Even in private life, it is a normal part of the relationship to create difficulties. Think about friendships, which also deserve to be called friendship because of the fact that you can tell each other the uncomfortable truth. Or think about dealing with children, who you sometimes have to harshly bring out of their comfort zone in order to help them learn to take care of themselves.

The image of perfection

The resistance of the 3rd Naikan question is rather high because you would like to see yourself with no downsides. We have an ideal image of ourselves, consciously or unconsciously, and want to keep this positive image intact.

It is correct and necessary to have an ideal image of yourself. Unfortunately, we overlook the fact that an ideal image is only a guide, a directional arrow, a compass. Because we can never meet this ideal image completely. It is therefore in the nature of things that we constantly founder at our own ideals. So we learn to balance the thin line between ideal and reality.

Take it in a sporty manner

The longer I practise Naikan, the more I am able to see the 3rd Naikan question as a sporting challenge. In sports, it is important to master different levels of difficulty. It's about learning and training. As a prerequisite, you need to analyse your capabilities, strengths, weaknesses and mistakes. What difficulties have I caused? How can I learn from this? How can I deal with it better? How can I more adequately act and react?

Redemption

Finally, there is the spiritual quality of the 3rd Naikan question. Spiritual experience is of the opinion that you do not discover yourself as a selfish individual, but rather as part of the universe as a whole. Specifically through the 3rd Naikan question, you experience yourself as a human being who has many unpleasant and ugly sides — yet other people and the world have given so much.

The Naikan founder Ishin Yoshimoto expressed it as follows[4]: "This disgraceful, depraved, vile 'I' should actually go through agony — but I am grateful that I can breathe here in peace."

Despite being such a selfish entity, despite being so flawed, you realize that you are still part of the whole and you receive everything that you need to survive. This paradox is experienced as redemption.

*Wisdom is
taking things as they are…
and accepting the inevitable.*

Michel de Montaigne

The darn 4th question, which loses it's power

1st Naikan question: **What has person X done for me? What have I received?**	*2nd Naikan question:* **What have I done for this person? What have I given?**
4th question (Naikan doesn't ask this one): What difficulties has this person caused me?	*3rd Naikan question:* **What difficulties have I caused this person?**

Wait a moment — there was still a fourth question.

Yes, of course there is also the so-called 4th Naikan question: What difficulties has person X caused me?

It is noteworthy that after the 1st question — What has person X done for me? The opposite question is asked thereafter — What have I done for person X?

After the 3rd question — What difficulties have I caused person X? — one is tempted to ask the question: What difficulties has person X caused me?

During Naikan one also remembers the situations in which other people caused you difficulties and problems. That is also part of life.

So why does Naikan not ask this question?

We know the 4th question far too well.

The reason why this 4th question is deliberately excluded in Naikan, is that our ego is constantly engaged with this issue in our daily life anyway. Examples come to mind extremely quickly.

In Naikan, one assumes that the person develops a high level of self-centeredness in the course of his or her development and a lot of power is used to make demands on the environment. If the environment or other people do not meet these expectations and requirements, then we say, "this causes me difficulties."

But does this get us anywhere?

Of course, other people or situations have caused us difficulties and problems. It is a valuable self-protection mechanism to recognize where actions are taken against our being or our interest. But we usually know this perspective very well. So why work on something again? It's like chewing on an old chewing gum.

Naikan does not say: The 4th question does not exist.

Naikan just says: Work on what you usually do not pay particular attention to. Work with the three Naikan questions. Because that is how you can focus your attention on what opportunities you have.

Making a mountain out of a molehill

It is unbelievable that X did that to me... It's outrageous that X did that... Why did X do that?... Just imagine what X did... Do you know that feeling when your thoughts continuously revolve around a particular situation? And we even include our friends and acquaintances in our problem?

We often make a mountain out of a molehill by holding on to negative thoughts. Has it ever contributed to a positive change when you have busied yourself with why someone has caused you difficulties? The answer is probably no. Because we ultimately cannot control the behaviour of other people. We have no power over other people, they just do what they want to.

We also harbour feelings of anger, rage, hatred, and helplessness when we deal with the things that other people or external circumstances have caused.

A practical test — think of a person who has caused you difficulties or problems recently.

Remember what this person did, or didn't do, what he did wrong, how unjust, negligent, or ignorant it was. How do you feel when you think about it? Do you feel good when doing so? Or does your mood drop drastically?

The 4th question shows what is not working or should have been done differently, what someone should or shouldn't have said or done… so you are looking at what 'isn't'. Naikan looks at what 'is'.

Wanting to change what cannot be changed

We run countless empty kilometres internally because we are trying to change what cannot be changed. If we constantly deal with situations where others have caused us difficulties or problems, then that's basically a waste of time and energy.

Of course we want to understand why the other person caused us difficulties. Sometimes it even helps if we understand others because we are thereby better able to accept what happened to us. However, that doesn't change anything. We want to make unpleasant experiences undone. Another desire that cannot possibly be fulfilled. A lot of effort for nothing.

And we would preferably like to tell the other person why they should change and cause us less problems. We cannot change someone else, that's impossible. As already mentioned: We have no power over other people, they just do what they want to.

Why does the 4th question have such power?

We humans have the tendency to only slightly perceive what is going well and running smoothly. However, if there is something unusual or a problem, then our attention is focused on it in a flash. We want to know immediately — what's going on? Where is the problem?

That is why many traditions teach mindfulness and equanimity. Mindfulness teaches you to see the inconspicuous things, all that is fine, that is running well and easily. Equanimity means not to immediately act out, but to remain calm, to accept the way things are, and then to take appropriate action.

These properties are not very popular in our culture of "action". In addition, we maintain a strong problem-oriented approach in our culture — what's the problem? What is the solution? What does one need to change? Here we see what "one" needs to change, not necessarily where change is possible — within ourselves.

There is nothing you can do

Because the other person did this or that, I can't... Because the other person is this or that way, I can't... Aren't those wonderfully convenient excuses? How about the killer phrase: There is nothing you can do.

We often use the 4th question as an excuse for one's own non-doing. Instead of looking at the facts and filtering one's own part, we prefer to stay in the belief that there is nothing we can do. After all, it is the other person's fault. These and other excuses[5] keep us from moving our attention away from others and towards ourselves.

However, with the 2nd and 3rd Naikan questions, Naikan asks: What have I contributed to the situation? I can deduce the following from this: What can I do? And not as a mere theory, but in connection with what actually happened.

Do I need to suppress the 4th question?

No, because everything that we suppress comes back with full force at some point. Take this view into account, but do not give the 4th question the power to suppress the other perspectives. The Naikan strategy is to disempower the 4th question by focusing on the three Naikan questions.

Internal and external observation

Naikan is about self-observation, looking inward. The 4th question is external observation, you are looking outward, observing the behaviour of others. Through self-observation it becomes clear how to behave yourself and which behavioural patterns one possesses. If you know and understand exactly how you think, speak and act, then you will be better able to make a difference in your life.

The key to change

Naikan assumes that the key to change is in each individual themselves. That means that one doesn't push the blame or the responsibility onto one's mother, one's partner, society, the system, and so on. But one takes responsibility oneself for how one lives.

This does not mean that you do not notice which mistakes other people make, which deficiencies occur in systems or institutions, and the like. Important for the purpose of Naikan is not to deal with the mistakes of others or the environment for hours, weeks, or years, but to recognize your own contribution and to effectively act on this basis.

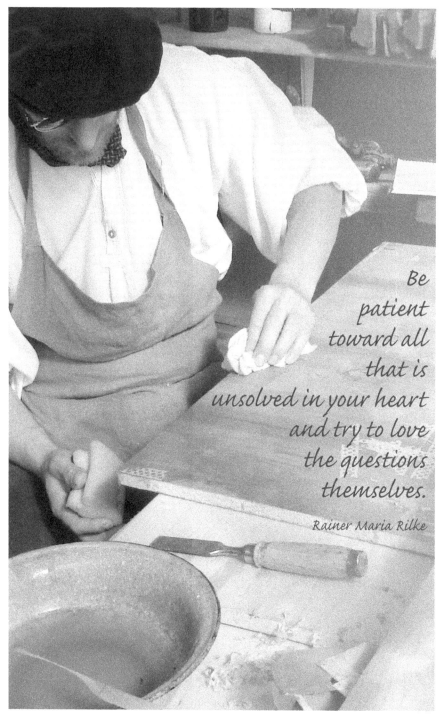

Three questions change you

No, you won't become a different person through Naikan. The change occurs in such a way that you get to know and accept yourself better, with all your strengths, weaknesses and flaws. And you also learn to accept other people, with all their strengths, weaknesses and flaws.

Ask the horse

In Naikan, we learn to see the facts. We recognize that what actually happens is not analogous with our desires, expectations, evaluations, thoughts, feelings, etc.

The following Zen story expresses this very well.[6] A man is sitting on his rapidly galloping horse. There is a man standing along the way, who shouts: "Where are you riding to so fast?" The rider replies, "I don't know! Ask the horse!"

Desires, expectations, evaluations, thoughts, feelings, etc. are valuable parts of our personality. They are our "horses". In order to keep the reins tight and control the direction, it is necessary to know the characteristics of the horse and to work with them.

Being an adult

The 1st Naikan question points to what other people have done for us. We recognize that our mother, father, partner, etc. did everything they could for us. With the 2nd and 3rd Naikan questions, we see how we have acted. We also did what we could. This allows you to break away from expectations and accusations that you have dragged with you up to now. Why condemn someone, or even yourself, just because they could not do the impossible?

As an adult, I can take the expectation-goggles off my face and see clearly.

After several years of Naikan practise, I'll never forget how I suddenly saw all kinds of pubescent people everywhere, regardless of whether they were 16, 36 or 56 years old. I observed behaviours along the lines of: "I'm right, regardless of what you say!" It was quite irritating to see that so many adults never behaved in an adult manner. Today, I can recognize that I myself sometimes still react like a rebellious pubescent teen, or a pouting toddler, in some situations. These behaviours are simply part of life. However, I am more aware of them and I'm working on primarily behaving like an adult.

What does it actually mean to behave like an adult?

Children experience that the world cares about their well-being. Adolescents experience that they have to learn to take care of themselves, and they fight for their place in the world. Being an adult means taking care of yourself because no one is responsible anymore.[7] Recognizing yourself and the world, acting in a self-determined way, being responsible for your own life with a positive attitude. As well as you can.

Accepting your life story

Being an adult also means facing everything that you have experienced, and accepting everything that you are now. In a Naikan retreat week, you can take on any unprocessed experiences and accept them as valuable parts of your being. At the end of her first Naikan retreat, a Naikan participant said: "It's as if I came here with a backpack full of heavy stones. Now the backpack is very light."

My perspective is not the only one

If you use the three Naikan questions to investigate situations and the contact to other people, then you will quickly come to a hurdle. First, you will answer quite naturally, how it corresponds to your own mind set. But slowly you begin to question things. Is this is also true for the other person? Or does it only look this way from my perspective?

A practical example from everyday life — 2nd Naikan question: What have I done for my co-worker? I explained a new work procedure to her.

Maybe I'm angry at her because she was not really listening. (This is usually where you stop exploring the situation in more detail, because you feel that you are in the right, and you are annoyed.) Well, the 4th question (What difficulties has my colleague caused me?) is left out in Naikan. If I look at the situation more closely, then I realize that I did not answer her questions, but simply explained according to my own logic. This means that I did indeed explain the new work procedure — 2nd Naikan question — but at the same time I caused her some difficulties — 3rd Naikan question. I did not adapt to her way of thinking.

From the Naikan approach, this implies that one explores the perspective of the other person. You gain an added perspective. Our own perspective is not necessarily wrong, but it is definitely not the only one, and certainly not the only correct one.

For this reason, there is a Naikan recommendation to see through the eyes of others. Don't answer the Naikan questions the way you yourself think, but rather try to answer as the other person thinks and feels — at least, as well as you know and can assess that person.

Freedom in giving and taking

Naikan is a method that makes you independent. The three Naikan questions give you a tool, which you always have with you. You can always keep a close eye on the giving and taking with this tool. The decision of how to deal with this is completely up to you.

Everything significant is uncomfortable.
Johann Wolfgang von Goethe

The importance of the three questions

The Naikan founder, Ishin Yoshimoto, recommended the following for the practise of Naikan: Use 20% of your time to reflect on the 1st Naikan question, 20% on the 2nd Naikan question and devote 60% of your time to the 3rd Naikan question.

Specifically the uncomfortable 3rd question has a powerful effect. With the 3rd question you cannot take refuge in an ideal world and you have to admit your own mistakes and weaknesses. If we acknowledge that we are not perfect, then that makes us human. And we thus lower our, often unrealistic, expectations.

In light of the three questions

It is important to look at one's experiences in light of all three Naikan questions, as this opens up the world of giving and receiving.

1st Naikan question: What has person X done for me?

The 1st Naikan question points to what I have received — regardless of whether I wanted it or not, or whether I deserved it or not. I got it. In order for me to not feel guilty about having received so much, there is the

2nd Naikan question: What have I done for person X?

Not only other people have given of themselves, but so have I — whether I was happy about it or not, whether it was voluntarily or not, the fact is that I gave something of myself. The first two Naikan questions often tempt us to only see the pleasant and beautiful things. Therefore, an additional perspective is needed — the

3rd Naikan question: What difficulties have I caused person X?

Yes, I am a person with less beautiful sides, a normal person, with lumps and bumps, someone who makes mistakes and causes difficulties. The key to change lies mostly in the 3rd Naikan question, because I have to perceive myself as a complete person, I have to look into the depth and feel what my actions have caused — comprehensively.

Is the 3rd question the most important?

My experience in Naikan has made me very flexible. Every person has different aspects, which are priorities to them.

I have experienced that for some people the 2nd Naikan question was very helpful, because they were able to perceive themselves as people acting of their own accord, rather than feeling helpless or unimportant. I then heard statements like: "For the first time I see myself as an endearing child."

For others the 1st Naikan question was important because they could see how much support they had received from other people. This made them feel rich and blessed, instead of living as if they were lacking something as they had done before. I then heard statements like: "The expectations that I had of my partner were so high that I didn't even see how much he was doing for me."

And for many people the 3rd Naikan question was the key to a better understanding of themselves and others. I then heard statements like: "I have never seen myself like this before. So many things are becoming clear now." Understanding when you have caused others difficulties, means that you maintain a more conscious overview of your own actions. You learn to distinguish between difficulties that you no longer want to cause, and difficulties that cannot be avoided. This brings clarity and more peace into the inner workings.

When I am guiding a Naikan group, I leave it up to the Naikan participants to decide how much time they want to spend on each Naikan question. However, I take care that not one of the three questions is omitted.

Does one always find answers in Naikan?

Sometimes yes, sometimes no. Both are possible. Naikan, itself, never gives answers – never, because Naikan is only a way of looking at things.

The answers can be found in yourself. In the busyness of everyday life, we often take too little time to conduct an internal dialogue and to see things more clearly. In the confusion of countless experiences, one always ends up at the question: What is it really about? If you use the Naikan questions in everyday life, you can trigger this process of inner clarity. What is your own part, what does the other person contribute to the situation?

To perform this inner dialogue more clearly, I recommend practising Naikan in silence. This makes it much easier to look at the different aspects that so often become blurred in everyday life, and which sometimes seem a complete mess in your head. In the structured Naikan practise, in a retreat week, the answers to the questions will come to you, as well as repeated "aha moments". One notices, for example, that one almost always reacts in a certain way and it's just a part of one's being, or one carries an experience with oneself and always responds according to the same pattern. These may be significant findings and could cause you not to be subsequently fazed by similar situations.

A question of ethics

By always focusing our attention on the reaction of other people, we get a more realistic estimate of our own behaviour. The reaction of the other person tells us whether we have caused a problem or not. The self-reflection not only makes us aware of how our behaviour has affected ourselves, but also how the other person views it.

Did I behave correctly? We frequently ask ourselves this question. The assessment of right and wrong needs a foundation, this foundation would be 'ethics'. Is someone being harmed because of me? How truthful am I? Do I take things without consent?

You will find answers to these questions with the 3rd Naikan question. Moreover, Naikan provides another exercise in order to examine the question of ethics in your behaviour. Namely, lying and stealing.

You can come to terms with your mistakes if you are strong enough to admit them.

François de La Rochefoucauld

Lying and stealing

A representation of Naikan without the topics of lying and stealing would not be complete. Because the founder of Naikan, Ishin Yoshimoto, attached great importance to ensuring that each Naikan participant examines themselves in light of:

LYING = not sticking to the whole truth

STEALING = taking something that was not given freely

Ishin Yoshimoto considered it to be so important, that he took this issue from the Buddhist practise[8] and applied it to the non-religious Naikan method. Working with the issue of lying and stealing is an integral part of a classic Naikan week.

Lying and stealing is part of any spiritual tradition, every culture, every social community. Ethics, whether spiritual or from social relationships, always concentrate on reducing lying and stealing. Naikan is an opportunity to focus on your own actions in relation to lying and stealing. Because what you can observe, you may also be able to influence.

No, not me!

You might be saying: "No, not me. I don't lie and I certainly don't steal. I am a good person."

Then I must tell you that everyone lies, and everyone steals. This is simply part of our nature, it is a natural part of being human. Not recognizing this means that you are lying to yourself. By doing so you are stealing your own opportunity to see through and be aware of your lying and stealing, and therefore being able to actively influence your actions.

Why is it so hard for us to see when we lie and steal?

Lying and stealing is prohibited!

Especially in Christian culture, we live in an environment which is strongly intertwined with feelings of guilt. If we lie or steal, or act against prevailing morality in any other way, we feel uncomfortably guilty. Because we are not allowed to lie and steal. We often go even one step further and hate ourselves for it. Maybe it has to do with a misguided sense of repentance that is held with one's own feelings of guilt. Fact is that we are often very tough on ourselves. Because we don't want to feel guilty, we simply forbid ourselves from making mistakes.

Unfortunately, this just doesn't work. Even if we forbid lying and stealing, we will never succeed entirely. Yes, we can and should lead a life with as little lying and stealing as possible. However, we will never be able to do it a hundred percent.

Naikan offers the opportunity to explore exactly in what way lying and stealing is present in one's life.

Lying and stealing: Naikan, only with the 3rd question

The approach of Naikan, with regard to the topic of lying and stealing, is to chronologically consider one's own biography in over viewable periods. For example, I begin with my first six years of life. What situations come to mind where I lied or stole? Where did I cause difficulties? Namely with regard to the specific perspective of lying and stealing:

LYING = not sticking to the whole truth
e.g. Not telling the truth
- Hiding something
- Manipulating others
- Generalizations
- "Yes" instead of "No"/ "No" instead of "Yes"
- ...

STEALING = taking something that was not given freely
e.g. Material things
- Time
- Attention

- Space
- Capabilities of others
- ...

Everything counts. Small things and large things. My actions, words, thoughts. It is about seeing where you have lied to someone or stolen from someone. Sometimes you observe where you have lied to, or stolen from, yourself.

Yes, it is uncomfortable to face these facts. I can only encourage you to examine these areas carefully because, as a result, you will be able to accept the uncomfortableness and thus become free internally.

Wash away the devil

The devil, what shall we do with him? If we send him away he will come back again. If we lock him up he will run around and break free. So what can we do with him? We can only wash him away.

These words of Zen Master Reiunken Shue Usami[9] have touched me deeply. Yes, the devil... my lying, my stealing, all the unhealthy, uncomfortable, destructive, negative sides of me. They were here, they are here, they will always be here. It doesn't matter if I turn away or if I suppress these parts of me. Because also these things are a part of my being. It's better if I take them on, come into contact with them, cleanse myself repeatedly. Wash away "my" devil...

Everyone has good and bad sides. Dealing with lying and stealing brings your own dark sides to light. You won't be a better person if you know and accept your bad sides, but it simply makes you more human.

Classic Naikan and multi-variant Naikan

The classic form of Naikan is practised over the period of one week. In this time, the three Naikan questions are applied to the essential people in your own life. Naikan weeks are usually held in specially equipped centres, but also in other appropriate venues or seminar centres.

In addition to the tried and tested Naikan week, Naikan can also be practised in different time periods: 1-day Naikan, a Naikan weekend, 5-day Naikan, Naikan retreat phases of two weeks or longer.

There are special offers where Naikan is combined with other methods, such as Kodo-Naikan (in combination with coaching, in a professional context), Naikan and Zen meditation, Naikan and meditative singing, Naikan and fasting, Naikan in motion (with short hikes)… The variety of Naikan combinations will probably continue to grow. Naikan can be independently used as a daily exercise in everyday life, either in addition to daily activities or in mini-breaks during the day. Also written Naikan, in the form of a Naikan diary, is an option.

Furthermore, there are offers of assistance from Naikan guides in everyday life, in the form of occasional or regular counseling in individual conversations, via telephone, e-mail or other means of communication.

Besides Naikan for individuals, there are also various offers for companies, establishments and therapeutic institutions.

Okay, so now to Naikan.

Naikan experiential report by Jan J.

I was at a Naikan week in Vienna with Johanna about 7 weeks ago. After the course, she asked me to write a short text and I agreed, under certain conditions. I have let these go now :) And what can I say?! First of all, it was wonderful how she cared for me, organized medication for me when I was sick, and just in general, she was always there when I needed her. For this, a big THANK YOU.

Okay, so now to Naikan. From the beginning I was very excited and elated, though I did not know why I wanted to go there, I just wanted to go. And then I just made the trip from Berlin.

I didn't perceive the environment as unusual — perhaps I am familiar with it through Zen.

However, being the only student was a new experience. But I got used to it quickly, and on the second night I wrote in my diary "being alone is cool", and that didn't change during the entire course.

The Naikan itself was a wonderful experience. By using the three questions and the given structure of life phases, I managed to see new perspectives, and some things simply ceased to exist. I saw myself more clearly and, at the same time, felt closer and more detached from the people I was focusing on.

My relationship to my family has become even more relaxed. It was amazing to see which glasses I had put on and still do. The introspection gave me great pleasure, even if it was not always easy. But due to the fact that a short conversation took place every 90 minutes, it was easier to stay in my rhythm.

I find it amazing to also use Naikan in everyday life. I find daily Naikan to be a great help. What has this day done for me? What have I done for this day? What difficulties have I caused today? This is applied to both the persons with whom I am in contact, as well as to the day in general. I can think of so many things for which I am grateful when I do Naikan, but they often go unnoticed otherwise. Be it the blue sky, the air we breathe, the breeze at the river, my room, noises, or other things. Or also with regard to the persons with whom I am in contact. It seems like being in a net. The cashier who is doing her job and smiled while doing it. Now I even find the act of ringing up my goods, even if the cashier is absent-minded, as something that she gives me. Or also the difficulties that I cause — I am much more aware of my responsibility through Naikan. Even if you only do themed Naikan for a few minutes, but several times a day, it's been helpful in my experience. So practising Naikan twice a week for 15 minutes is already helpful. So, now I have briefly touched on my experiences with Naikan in everyday life.

The interesting thing about Naikan is also playing with the different perspectives. The first-person perspective, the other person's perspective, the we-perspective, and the "objective" perspective, and millions of other perspectives, which can actually be omitted. Training this skill allows you to sensitize dealing with people in everyday life. I think it is then easier to distinguish between 'mine' and 'yours'.

Apart from that, I can sum up by saying that Naikan helps me to be more conscious of myself and my responsibility. It also helps me to be aware and appreciate my relationships more, and to be more tolerant and friendly to myself.

Written by Jan J. from Berlin in 2010. At the time he was taking part in a Naikan week in 2010 (Individual Naikan), at the age of 26, as a student nearing graduation, writing his thesis.

The Naikan technique and the Naikan depth effect

Naikan is a simple method — one only needs three questions, a clear mind and the willingness to see oneself. I call the basic tool of the three questions the "Naikan technique", which can be easily applied at any time.

However, if you want to experience Naikan in all its depth, then it takes more than just the Naikan technique. This dimension of Naikan can only be experienced through the combination with a period of silence and seclusion — one week is a minimum requirement. The "Naikan depth effect" is my term for the complex insight into the depths of life and of being, which is possible through the practise of Naikan.

Naikan technique	Naikan depth effect
3 Naikan questions	3 Naikan questions and retreating into silence (ideal: 1 week)
Focus on one person (or one topic) and a specific period of time	Focus on one person (or one topic) and a specific period of time and follow your biography chronologically
	Gentle, respectful accompaniment and short interviews

Naikan technique

In order to implement the Naikan technique, it is sufficient to focus on one person (or one topic) and a specific period of time, then what you have experienced with regard to that person (or topic), and ask the three Naikan questions. For example — my partner, in the period of last month. 1. What did my partner do for me in the course of last month? 2. What did I do for my partner? 3. What difficulties did I cause my partner last month?

This is a simple technique to get clarity as to who contributed what in this relationship. You can also use the Naikan technique to work through a particular situation or to develop a new perspective on a problem and its solution.

However, it is unlikely that you can work through deeper issues with the Naikan technique alone. Because those issues usually need much more time and peace to come up to the surface.

Naikan depth effect

If you have experienced Naikan in the tranquillity of a retreat, then you will not only connect Naikan with the question technique, but also automatically with inner peace, which is strengthened in a retreat.

Especially in a world of constant bustle, it is an advantage to practise Naikan in silence and seclusion. Deeper internal aspects can only be felt in silence and over a longer period of time. Water can only become clear if it is not constantly swirled around by wind and weather. Inner truths can only be understood if the inner workings are not constantly shaken up by the turbulences of everyday life.

You can work through your life story in a very structured manner in seclusion. You do not only focus on a person (or topic) and a specific time period. You also follow your biography chronologically and bring certain time periods to light with the 3 Naikan questions. In this way, you can bring some order into your life, your life will be more clearly visible through your memories, and individual events find their place in the whole.

Overly powerful memories lose their power, seemingly insignificant events turn out to be pioneering, forgotten memory treasures come to light.

Through the external silence, inner peace can occur. Perception is intensified through the peacefulness. The fullness of life becomes conscious. You yourself control your own introspection, and thereby experience yourself as self-determined person. And you get to experience that you are not alone, because the Naikan guides are there for you and give you support the entire way.

Naikan begins with the mother

Your life began because your mother gave birth to you. That is why your mother is the first person you focus on in a Naikan retreat. If you didn't grow up with your birth mother, then you look at the person who took on the mother role. After you have examined your life with regard to the relationship with your mother, you usually examine your life with regard to your father.

Your parents are the people who have given you your life. Your mother and father have done many things right, and they have made many mistakes. In Naikan, you can take a close look at the image you have of your parents. Does the image that you have of your mother or father withstand the Naikan examination? Or do the facts alter your existing subjectively-coloured image?

Memories that were particularly beautiful or painful make a deep imprint on your memory. We assemble an image of a person based on these memorable experiences, for example of our mother and father. Countless other things disappear in the depths of your memory.

We recall, for example, the fact that our mother cooked a dish that we hated. But we forget that our mother cooked every day and that we actually enjoyed most of the meals. Or we remember that our father was not at home very often. But we forget that he was away because he had been working in order for us to have a roof over our heads and to have enough money for food, clothes and school trips.

Naikan is about bringing these forgotten memories out again. In this way, the overpowering memories are put in a proper place and the many seemingly unimportant memories make up a more complete and realistic picture of the past. And above all, it becomes conscious that we have created a subjective image of our mother or father, or any other person, which does not necessarily correspond to reality.

Setting it straight

In a Naikan retreat you examine your entire life story in relation to the fundamental relationships in your life. In addition to your parents, this also includes other people from your immediate family, such as siblings or grandparents, as well as other important people in your life, such as your own children, or people in your professional life.

So you are setting your internal life straight, comprehensively and in-depth. A Naikan week is therefore often referred to as internal "spring cleaning".

From 'what' to 'how'

At the beginning of Naikan you may think that it is primarily about the content. What have I experienced with my mother (or another person)? The memories and stories seem to be important.

At some point you realize that it is not solely about the memories and stories. The crucial part is not what you remember, but rather how you remember, how the memories arise, how you classify your experiences. The Naikan question is not: What have I experienced? The Naikan questions are: What has X done for me?

What have I done for X? What difficulties have I caused X? Through the practise of Naikan, the focus shifts from 'what' to 'how'. Naikan teaches you that it is important how you classify and processes the experienced. The question of what you experienced with your mother (or someone else), so the memory per se, is no longer in focus. Furthermore, with Naikan observation, you filter the facts from the memories and don't build any stories or explanations around them.

From working through it, to perceiving it

Of course, many people come to Naikan because they want to deal with something that happened in the past, or because they want to work through a topic to solve a problem.

Naikan is very helpful here — partly by working with the Naikan questions, but even more so by being at peace. If your inner being is at peace, then it is sufficient to simply be present and perceive the fullness of just being. New perspectives no longer develop, but they simply appear.

While practising Naikan you will have 'aha moments' and insights, by which one is overwhelmed and deeply touched. The practise continues and things always turn out differently than expected. Finally, Naikan becomes unspectacular as inner peace is the norm.

Practise makes perfect — still

When it comes to physical skills, such as sports, no one questions that it takes daily exercise in order to improve and be able to perform well. As soon as it comes to inner qualities and abilities, it is strangely supposed to happen very quickly — preferably in a consultation hour, a seminar weekend, or a short workshop.

Fast and effective, that is how it should be with the acquisition of social skills, communication skills, inner balance and happiness. What is obvious in sport, also applies to your inner being: it takes regular exercise and practise. New insights or skills must become second nature so that they are available in any situation of everyday life.

It is true that new perspectives or theoretical knowledge about a different behaviour can be attained quickly. However, the implementation of theory into practise takes practise.

A Naikan participant compares playing tennis to practising Naikan, and says that a Naikan week is like a tennis camp, where you intensively train and develop new skills. But if you do not continue to practise playing tennis after the camp, then you will lose the skills again. If you want to achieve lasting results, then you simply need practise.

The power of silence

Naikan is always practised individually. When attending a retreat, each participant practises alone in a private area, either in a group room or in a single room. Naikan is about retreating from everyday life and having undisturbed dialogues with oneself.

There are no group activities, with the exception of the introductory meeting at the beginning, and the concluding discussion at the end of the Naikan week.

The entire week is spent in silence, thus there is no contact with the other Naikan participants or the outside world. Discussions exclusively take place with the Naikan guides, where you have the opportunity to speak about your Naikan experiences eight to ten times a day.

The best suited venue for such a retreat is a quiet place where there is as little noise as possible and no other disturbances. Peace of mind is supported through the quiet environment.

Can one endure that?

One week of not speaking — can one even endure that? This question is asked frequently. It's no wonder, as so many people are not aware of the soothing power of silence because of the noisy world we live in.

I can honestly say, from years of experience, that one week of silence is easily endurable. The adjustment is easier than you might think. Moreover, the silence is soon experienced as pleasant.

"If I can do it, anyone can!" This statement came happily and repeatedly from a Naikan participant during her Naikan week. She had had great concern whether she would be able to endure the week of silence. As a manager of a large company, it was part of her job to travel to various locations around the world, she had to be available day and night, even on holiday she constantly played with her BlackBerry. She endured the week, and it was easier than she had thought.

It is not only silence

To calm those of you down, who cannot imagine a week in silence, there are brief discussions with the Naikan guides several times a day. Therefore, it is not completely silent for a whole week because you have private talks every day, at intervals of one to two hours.

However, it is of importance that you do not have contact with the other participants or the outside world. Because each and every Naikan participant — you included — has the right to a safe space in which he or she can deal with themselves in an undisturbed manner.

The silence and the quiet sounds

What is the point of retreating and being silent when it comes to Naikan? Firstly, the power of concentration increases so that memories can come up to the surface more easily. Secondly, the retreat offers a safe space to experience and accept rising thoughts and emotions.

Quiet sounds, that one would otherwise ignore, come into perception through the silence. This applies to the quiet sounds from your own inner world, as well as to those from the environment. Although it sometimes seems that these sounds were not there before, they were always there, they were just not observed in everyday life or were intuitively included into an action. You will experience that communication arises despite the silence. This also happens in everyday life. In Naikan you can more consciously perceive this form of communication that takes place without words.

Being alone — with yourself, and the world

If you practise being alone with yourself, then you will better be able to cope with forced situations of solitude. Many people suffer from loneliness, so it's good to learn how to deal with being alone. Naikan is an opportunity to independently and consciously deal with oneself and the world.

Being a human being is a paradox — on one hand, the person is an individual and has to accept that he is a separate person. On the other hand, one is always and without exception involved in the whole, in a particular way, no matter how passive you stay or how actively you engage others. You can learn these two levels of individuality and connectedness in Naikan.

Absolute silence — not really possible

Honestly, I have not yet found a place where there is absolute silence, and especially not over a longer period of time. Sounds either come from nature, from the technological world, from our neighbours, from other Naikan participants, etc… you cannot really stop life.

Of course, Naikan guides strive to find quiet places to practise Naikan. However, there are no perfect conditions anywhere. There have been the funniest (or most disturbing, depending on how you look at it) situations in Naikan. For example, a seminar house in the mountains, only nature surrounding it, where a tree was being cut down exactly behind the house, or a quiet monastery where a weekend marquee was being set up in the neighbouring meadow for political speeches, music and a bouncy castle…

The best is to be aware that there will not be absolute silence at a Naikan retreat, but it will be a quieter environment than you're used to in everyday life.

Meditation about the bunk, in my 1ˢᵗ Naikan week.

Naikan experiential report by Werner F.

I have to say goodbye to you, you little room.
You reminded me of a grave when I saw you for the first time:
so narrow, so tight. But I felt so comfortable in you, so fast.
Like being in a womb.
That is what Klaus, our cook, said during the briefing.
And it's true. You surrounded me, comforted me, protected me. But from what? The environment was not hostile, but comfortable, quiet, friendly.
It was exciting, an instant anticipation when I heard Johanna come closer. I felt her concentration in front of the sliding door. She pushed it open a bit: "Are you ready for a conversation?", she smiled at me with a beaming face. I sat down at the door and read to her.

Yes, dear room, you wrapped me up in my happy moments (luck in love, luck in friendship, first years of having children…).
You laughed when I told utterances from children's mouths, you shared my worries and saw my tears (there were not as many as I had feared, but they were bitter enough).
Yes, my dear room, you are STUFFED WITH MY LIFE!
How is it now? Does it stay in you or will it be "aired out"?
No — I'll take everything home with me.
You saw me write for many hours — my hand hurt.
But I realized over time that it was gold flowing out of my pen,
the GOLD OF MY LIFE.
I scooped as much as I could from the treasure chest of my life.
I, impatient person, came to rest IN YOU.

I could not stand the permanent sitting — I had to get out.
How beautiful the weather was outside, how beautiful the meadow was.
This single layer — as I saw it — fit perfectly to Naikan.
Well rested, I took my "shovel" in hand and continued to dig.

It was gratifying to see what treasures came to light.
"All of this is IN YOU!" So much is not yet known, is still hidden.
I am aware of what I have dug up,
I carry it in my hands;
And if trouble comes my way,
I'll take the book in hand
and read from it:
From girth, suffering and utter pleasure…
I've found my happiness!
So live well you narrow room,
I'll speak of you often,
So people will come here to you,
Tormented by stress and worry.
Let them dig for many hours,
Into the Gold of their lives.
Then the mouth may say:
It was probably nothing — nothing at all — in vain!
Life is sometimes pleasure, sometimes suffering,
Sometimes work and sometimes a break.
Now I will pack my things
and go home RICH.

Written in 2004 after a Naikan week (Naikan in a private bunk in the group room). Mr. F. is a retired teacher.

Creating order in your inner being

Naikan creates order and structure in several ways:

- You focus on one person in your life.
- You observe what you have experienced with this person in a Naikan retreat, chronologically from the first time you had contact until today (or until the last contact).
- You match the memories to the 3 Naikan questions.

In dealing with the past, certain situations usually come to mind, which have been imprinted into your memory. Very often these are painful memories, but also exceptionally beautiful events become readily available to us.

Already at this point Naikan invites us to look at the past in a different manner; Not only the special events should come into mind, but also the everyday, unspectacular, usually unnoticed experiences should be remembered. In this way, some spectacular events lose power and seemingly unimportant experiences become more important. The experiences can be classified differently and can find a proper place in your inner being. The puzzle pieces of our memories come together more and more, to form a clear picture of your own life path.

Focusing on one person

Because our memory stores the experience as a complete package, we remember a situation with all the individuals involved and all the appertaining circumstances.

The situation looks something like this in our heads: person A did this, person B reacted in this way, person C said that, person D later… As a rule, our thoughts spin around a particular situation, we make connections, we try to understand what happened.

Naikan operates differently. You focus on one person and leave out memories which concern other people. You are not looking for explanations, are not researching the causes, are not looking for contexts or consequences.

What have I experienced with this person? With this, you open the package that is stored in your memory and bring those elements into consciousness, which deal with that specific person. It is not rare that you will realize that you have given this person a much bigger (or smaller) part in the situation than the facts actually demonstrate on closer inspection. Looking closely at a single person, and the facts, makes it possible to process the experience and possibly reorganize it.

Follow your own life story chronologically

Remembering one's life from the beginning to the present in chronological order, that is what differentiates Naikan from other methods. Many other methods, just like Naikan does, look at the experienced, work through memories, and deal with those people who have played a role in your life.

Naikan considers it important to go through the memories from the first encounter with a person (or topic), to the last contact with this person (or topic), time period for time period. No chains of association, no crosslinks, and no complex relationships are researched or focused on. On the contrary, Naikan reduces the complexity of memory by focusing on one person and each phase of life.

In a sense, the memories and time periods are lived through again. However, it is not about the mere restaging of events. You also do not regress to being the person you were at that time, even if feelings and thoughts of the past come up.

So that you are not overwhelmed by memories, Naikan has several protection mechanisms. An important mechanism is the meta-level: the perspective of the adult you are now, always runs simultaneously. Although you get in touch with your memories very intensively, the inward observer remains present at all times. This allows some things to consciously or unconsciously be understood or processed in retrospect. The tools of internal observation are the 3 Naikan questions.

Matching your experiences to the 3 Naikan questions

The 3 questions are the core of Naikan. They allow you to stop your own thought patterns or spirals at any time.

One participant gave the following feedback: "I have never consciously experienced such a deep concentration. Especially after my depression, which was accompanied by persistent rumination and being plagued by automatic thoughts, I experienced having a power over my thoughts through Naikan, which has given me so much strength."

The 3 Naikan questions strengthen one's personal skills and bring order into your inner being. What has the other person done for me, what is his part? And what is my part, what did I do, what difficulties have I caused?

Spring cleaning your inner world

Naikan can be compared to an internal spring cleaning. Your own inner world is trawled through, sorted out, and cleaned, down to the smallest detail. Memories are found and tested with the 3 Naikan questions. Outdated and useless thoughts and feelings are sorted out. Useful things are (re)discovered and (newly) appreciated.

A Naikan participant wrote the following to me after her Naikan week: "In the first days after my return I was so happy and joyous, that my husband said he would send me to a Naikan retreat every year! I really do feel lighter and happier."

*We don't receive wisdom;
we must discover it for ourselves
after a journey that no one
can take for us or spare us.*

Marcel Proust

Gentle, respectful accompaniment

During a Naikan retreat you are accompanied by trained Naikan guides. Naikan accompaniers are responsible for ensuring that you are undisturbed and that you are supplied with everything you need.

Although you will spend the majority of the time alone in your practise area, you are not left alone. One could say that the reception area is open 24 hours a day at a Naikan retreat. If questions arise, you are more than welcome to simply voice them. You will receive support and possible recommendations.

The discussed issues are, of course, treated confidentially.

The daily routine leaves ample time and space for dialogues; The periods of silence take up most of the time. At any time — day and night — there is someone available for you to speak to about urgent or unusual matters. Naikan guides individually accompany each person in self-examination, and provide a framework so that you can perceive your own potentials and mistakes in order to learn from them.

Your own individual responsibility is paramount. Every person knows their own life best. Therefore, Naikan guides do not push you, but rather respect your individual pace and the personal way in which you handle practising Naikan.

Naikan accompaniers do not judge, praise, criticize, demand, or push you… They simply listen, consciously, with wholehearted attention, with mind and heart. Everything that comes up is allowed.

Gentle

One often reads that Naikan is a "gentle method" or a "gentle way" to self-knowledge. Naikan is gentle because it stimulates self-reflection, but does not force it. Naikan is gentle because it does not specify the direction of knowledge, but it indicates a way of practising. Naikan is gentle because the Naikan guides accompany you gently and intervene in your introspection as little as possible.

The reserved manner of the Naikan guides may come across as "cold". It is not always easy to take responsibility of oneself. People practising Naikan ask themselves: "Am I doing everything right?" Naikan guides do not judge, they do not say "well done!". They just respect the individual path of each participant.

Respectful

The personal pace, the individual memories and the unique way of life of each human being is respected.

The mere fact that a person gathers the time and courage to examine themselves intensively, deserves consideration and respect. The questions of participants are heard and the response is usually the encouragement to find an answer yourself. That's why Naikan guides often say that it is less about leading and more about accompanying.

Accompaniment

You, as a Naikan participant, go through your life internally again, see new perspectives through Naikan, and can organize the experienced events in a better way. Naikan guides will accompany you on this journey.

The biggest temptation when guiding Naikan is the following thought: "I know what's best for this Naikan participant." Because accompanying in Naikan, means trusting the participant to recognize the best for him or herself.

Life is beautiful!

Naikan experiential report by Barbara S.

I am 58 years old, have three children, and changed pretty much everything in my life 3 years ago.

I was supposed to take a job as a commercial director, received executive coaching, and everything should go its way. But this coaching sparked changes in me. I had always worked hard, had always been there for everyone else, had taken care of everybody. Of my children, my husband. It was okay — but where was I with my desires, my needs, my future? I had completely lost myself in this regard in the last few years, could only be slightly grateful. I just didn't feel myself anymore.

I suddenly felt that something had to change. But what? I wanted to feel my strength from the inside — or was I already feeling it? I wanted more access to myself. Inside, I felt like I was torn, yet powerful. After talking to my coach, I decided to go to the Swiss Alps for two months and to help out in a mountain inn as a temp. I quickly received an offer, took the entire vacation time that I had stored up, and several additional unpaid days, and drove through the night into the mountains.

It was a beautiful time, but also a very stressful time. After almost 2 months, I knew that I had to listen to my heart and have faith in myself. My heart is my guide.

In the following months I changed a lot in my life. Every day it was something else. It was not easy. I was afraid, it was hard to let go. Nevertheless, I quit my job, left my husband and my beloved house with the beautiful garden, and moved to Switzerland with two suitcases.

I got an apartment and took temp jobs. A really nice time began. I met a lot of nice people, and I also got to know myself again. But I still temporarily had huge existential fears, and old patterns came up again, as well as the good old topic of "confidence in myself " — self-confidence. This upheaval challenged me greatly. I had already let go of so much, but I reached my limits again and again.

I kept consistent contact with my coach and told him how I was feeling. After I had, once again, lost sight of what I should be grateful for every day, he turned my attention to Naikan. I concerned myself with it and decided, in a short time, to practise Naikan with Johanna in Vienna.

On my way to Johanna, I had a lot of concerns about the upcoming time, about the silence, about coming closer to myself. I was curious and excited. How would I do there? Would I be able to live without communication to the outside world? Without my mobile phone, without my laptop?

Then I arrived at Johanna's and was welcomed very warmly. After a delicious lunch and the introductory meeting, I began to focus on my mother and asked myself, in a highly concentrated manner, the three Naikan questions in four year time periods, until she left my life.

In the beginning I couldn't think of much. How was I supposed to remember a time so long ago? Then a bit more arose from my memory, and the more I looked into it, the more intense feelings became. I had never previously considered my mother in this way. In particular, the question of what difficulties I had caused her, was very hard for me. But with a memory of a really beautiful time, I realized the difficulties I had caused her, and felt improbable gratitude and love.

I felt the same about my father, my brother, my three children, my husband, from whom I had separated, and about the consideration of my life path. I changed my perspectives and realized that I had put too many expectations on the people around me, on life and everything else, and had experienced the resulting disappointment, and that life was a constant give and take. I realized how many beautiful moments I had experienced and how little I had seen them.

Particularly impressive to me was using the three Naikan questions with regard to my dark sides, such as lying and manipulating. I had never seen myself like that before. I suddenly realized how many times I had stolen in my life, how many times I had lied and cheated, or even exercised power over somebody. I was able to suddenly perceive and accept the feelings, reconcile with myself, develop a different awareness of my actions, and clearly took on more responsibility for my life.

For me, the Naikan week was an adventurous, exciting, exhausting, pioneering, but also humorous journey into my inner being.

After returning to my everyday life, I realized that I was facing people and everyday situations in a more relaxed and loving manner. I have become much happier and more grateful, I appreciate the little things in life. I approach alleged problems completely differently. Yes, Naikan has found a place in my life and I am very grateful for that.

I am looking forward to practising another week of Naikan and to beginning my training as a Naikan guide with Johanna. To you, dear Johanna, I just want to say thank you so much for your loving, spacious, non-judgmental and caring support in this Naikan week. I salute you.

Written in 2013 about the Naikan week (individual Naikan) in Vienna.

*Man may do and suffer,
but whatever it may be, he always and
inalienably possesses divine dignity.*

Christian Morgenstern

Everything is allowed

Naikan doesn't judge you. It doesn't matter what you have experienced, it has already happened. It's part of your past and thus part of the present. If you look at the past, then you have the possibility to see the experienced events from different perspectives. Perhaps you may recognize learning experiences, which you gathered through negative events. The more diverse your view of the past becomes, the more it sharpens your perspective of the present, and the more diverse your options for the future become.

Being perceived as a person

Everything, which appears, is allowed — through this basic attitude of the Naikan guides, people get the courage to show what the facts actually are, that's because they feel the respect and recognition of their being. Today, researchers of the brain know the following: "The efforts of the person to be seen as a human being is still more significant than what is commonly seen as the self-preservation instinct."[10]

I can only confirm this from my experience as a Naikan guide. It's not about my opinion; The effectivity and healing comes from really listening, if possible, without judging or commenting. For me, as a Naikan guide, the requirement for really listening is the sincere interest in people. I see this unique person who is sitting across from me and is sharing his or her unique way of seeing the world with me.

More listening than talking

A Naikan conversation is all about that Naikan guide listening. Sometimes a dialogue arises, but that is the exception. Many people appreciate the basic structure of the Naikan method, where conversations of only a few minutes take place, so that the practise of Naikan is disturbed as little as possible. Some people say that voicing what is thought gives them even more clarity. Sometimes people have a deep need to express themselves, because I hear "I cannot tell anyone else this" very often. Naikan guides have a sympathetic ear for any topic, regardless of how emotional, unusual or simple it may seem.

Findings simply arise

Through concentrated Naikan work, you come into deep contact with yourself. The Naikan method sets out clear structures, you focus on one person and one time period at a time. Despite this "limited" view, or perhaps because of it, new insights and perspectives come to life suddenly and unexpectedly.

Neither you, as Naikan participant, nor I, as Naikan guide, can predict when or even what findings will arise.

Insights or new perspectives often arise regarding people, topics, or events that are in focus in Naikan at that moment. But sometimes I have the impression that it doesn't matter which topic or person one is focusing on, knowledge and findings just make themselves visible.

As an example I would like to report on day-Naikan. The Naikan participant, a professional musician and someone who travels a lot, chose the topic of traveling for Naikan. She found many things, for example that someone always helped carry her heavy luggage, that the plane always landed safely — all the little and big things of everyday travel. In the last conversation of the Naikan day she reported, in quiet clarity, that she had now understood that life was preparation for death.

It was like driving from city A to city B on a train. No matter what she does on the train, the train will always arrive at train station B. The train of life always arrives at death. It is up to her how she behaves in the train of life.

It seems as if knowledge is literally waiting for the next best opportunity to finally show itself. I have experienced that often, and it still surprises me every time.

I presented my life as an exhibit,
I take the pain in stride.
One week in a tiny space,
And my life begins again with pride.

Memories resurface,
The joy and hate is mixed, this is no fable.
The only thing that counts is respect,
I lay my cards open on the table.

I wrote and drew this in a Naikan week in 2010. This was the best Birthday present that I have ever given myself. Thank you so much. Valentina

3. Naikan — How does such a retreat work?

Depending on the Naikan centre and the venue of the Naikan retreat, the conditions are designed differently. Inform yourself of the environment in advance.

Naikan can be practised in a group room with private training areas, or in a single room. Some venues are located in the countryside, surrounded by nature that gives you energy, some are located in the city.

There are dates on which many people are practising Naikan at the same time, and dates which you can book for private/single Naikan.

Regardless of the venue, and regardless of how many people are practising Naikan, the organizational flow of things has a basic structure.

The sequence of a Naikan retreat:

- Arrival at a Naikan venue, where you are welcomes in person.
- You move into your space/room where you will practise Naikan.
- If you have to do something before you go into the retreat, then you will be asked to do so before you begin Naikan (e.g. telephone calls, e-mails…). As you shouldn't have any distractions during the retreat.
- There is usually a joint meal before Naikan starts. This allows first introductions in a relaxed atmosphere.
- At the beginning there is an introduction, in which the conditions will be discussed and the Naikan method is presented with regard to form and content. Questions are answered.
- After the introduction, the Naikan exercise begins. As a sign that the retreat, the silence and the tranquillity have begun, a gong sound is usually heard.
- During the Naikan retreat the following has been agreed on: silence among everyone, no outside contact, no forms of media (no television,

radio, music, reading, computer, Internet), and this until the end of the retreat.
- It is recommended that you spend as much time on your Naikan space. Going outside is allowed, but should be kept to a minimum.
- There is no prescribed stance or posture in Naikan. You can sit, lie down, stand, head stand… You can also do exercises in between. If other participants are practising Naikan in the same room, you will be asked to be quiet.
- All meals are eaten in silence. The food is usually brought to your Naikan space on a tray. Fruit, tea and drinks are available throughout the day.
- Naikan is practised individually on your private Naikan space or in a single room. There are about 8-10 Naikan phases per day. The phases refer to the individual Naikan reflection sessions of 60-90 minutes on your own, and thereafter the private Naikan conversations with the Naikan guides. The private Naikan conversation is usually short (5-10 minutes).
- The daily routine at Naikan (varies depending on the Naikan centre):
    * Day beings at 7am, get up, bathroom time, then
    * beginning of the Naikan exercise,
    * breakfast at about 8am, then
    * continue with the Naikan exercise until the 1st individual Naikan discussion with the Naikan guide at about 9am (= 1st Naikan phase)
    * a total of 3 Naikan phases in the morning,
    * lunch at around 1pm,
    * 3-4 Naikan phases in the afternoon,
    * dinner at about 6pm,
    * 2-3 Naikan phases in the evening,
    * day ends at around 10pm.
- In some Naikan centres it is customary to perform about 30 minutes of work meditation once a day.
- At the end of the retreat, the formal structure and the silence end.
- After the silence has ended, there is a communal concluding discussion.
- Conclusion, usually with a meal or tea/coffee.
- Departure.

Practising Naikan at a retreat

At a Naikan retreat you will examine your own life story in a structured and deep manner. You will focus on a person or topic, and arrange the events using the Naikan questioning technique.

The practise of Naikan generally begins with the focus on the mother or the person who took on the role of the mother. You proceed chronologically and focus on the first period of your pre-school years, when you were 0-7 years old. You look at specific events which you can remember and always ask the three Naikan questions:

1st Naikan question: What did this person do for me in this time?
2nd Naikan question: What did I do for this person in this time?
3rd Naikan question: What difficulties did I cause this person in this time?

After each 60-90 minute period of reflection, the Naikan guide will come to you for your individual Naikan conversation. Thereafter you will explore the memories in the next period of about 4 to 6 years, e.g. focusing on your mother during the period of your elementary school when you were 7-11 years old, thereafter 11-15 years old and so on, until the present day (or if your mother is no longer alive, up to the day she passed away).

In this way, you structure the memories from the first encounter with this person up to the present time, or up to the time when the person left your life.

Depending on how old you are, you will spend one day, for example, focusing on your mother. Then you practise Naikan with the focus being on your father, your siblings, your grandparents, your partner, your own children, friends, colleagues, and specific topics… Which people and topics are focused on, is different for each individual.

Retreat, silence and comfort

In classic Naikan you can treat yourself to a real break. Worrying about nothing else but yourself — what a blessing! For one whole week there is no reading, no listening to the radio, no television, no phone, no computer, no contact with people outside Naikan. It is much easier to observe your inner being without external distractions and in the safety of a secure environment.

Retreating and being offline — is that even possible?

I am often asked: How will I be able to handle the silence? How can I cope without any communication from the outside world? How does that work, being offline for a week, without a phone or Internet?

If you have not yet had the experience of retreating for a few days, then you may have similar concerns. How can I manage without certain familiar things (be it sports, the outdoors, communication…)?

All I can say is that it is, of course, a change. But experience has shown that the study of one's own inner world is so fascinating that these concerns are hardly, or not at all, an issue during the week. You adapt. And a week is not that long. Moreover, retreating is perceived as pleasant very soon. Naikan participants are always amazed that they have no desire to make contact with the outside world after a few days. Because it's just thrilling to explore the diversity of your own inner world.

Silence — what's the point?

Naikan is a method in which you ask yourself questions and find your own answers. You will not find the answers by talking or through joint group exercises, but through self-reflection. That is why a Naikan retreat is a silent week, in which you do not communicate with other participants or outsiders. It is not about ignoring the other participants, but about showing them appreciation by respecting their practise space.

Your own answers to the questions are central in Naikan. Dealing with other people or things would merely distract or interfere with your own findings. Stay focused on yourself, nothing else is needed.

Comfort — in such a small space?

As further support for the introspection, the Naikan space which is assigned to you to practise, is usually quite small. If you practise Naikan in the group room you will have a private area behind a screen. If you practise in a single room, then that room is your home for a week.

No, you will not get claustrophobic because you feel constrained, don't worry. The small room gives you security and comfort. Some Naikan participants snuggle up in a blanket to feel even more comfortable. We humans like to retreat into protected corners where we feel safe. Think about small children. They crawl under the bed and pull another blanket in front of them. They don't do that because they want to lock themselves away or hide, they do it because the small cave gives them a feeling of protection and security. It is similar with the Naikan bunk.

You can, of course, leave your Naikan space at any time, you are never locked up. If there is a garden, you can go outside. If you have a single room, you can do exercises for your body in between. You can feel safe and free.

Isn't that boring?

Sitting around all day and thinking about your own life — isn't that boring?

No. If you manage to focus on the Naikan exercise, then it's not boring. You are observing your inner being. Boredom may arise in Naikan if you don't focus on your memories and the 3 Naikan questions.

Of course there are moments or phases of boredom during Naikan exercise. That can happen, just as it does from time to time in everyday life.

Or is there action, fun and excitement in your life at every moment? Would you even be able to stand it if every moment was filled with action, fun and excitement?

In everyday life we often don't notice when boredom or other feelings and needs arise. Because there is always some form of distraction from our inner life: talking, eating, watching TV, surfing the Internet, playing sports… In a Naikan retreat you can consciously perceive which feelings and needs emerge in us, in this case, for example boredom. The Naikan recommendation is: Just direct your attention back to practising Naikan.

Being cared for

There is another factor contributing to the fact that you will feel safe and comfortable in a Naikan retreat: the Naikan guides. They are the ones that provide the all-round care, the meals and so on. They always have a sympathetic ear for your concerns and provide assistance when needed. And when you have a private conversation, the Naikan guides will listen attentively and with appreciation.

Organizing your own life story: Biography work

Naikan proceeds in a structured manner. One goes through one's own life story several times, and matches experiences with the 3 Naikan questions. As a recurring theme there is a relationship with a specific person. In the beginning the mother is usually the focus of attention. This is followed by other caregivers or also other topics. Who or what is focused on in Naikan, is decided in the conversation with the Naikan guide.

How can I remember?

Internally turn your attention to the life period, which is being focused on in Naikan, examine memories related to the person and arrange the memories with regard to the 3 Naikan questions.

Some tips to recalling memories, for example, with the focus being on your mother in the first years of life. Where did I live at that time? Was it in the city, on the countryside? Was it an apartment, a house, and what did the rooms look like at the time? Where did I enjoy playing, in the house or outside? Where did I sleep? Where was the kitchen, who cooked? How were special occasions like a birthday, Christmas, Easter? What was the daily routine? Who woke me up, who prepared the breakfast, who brought me to kindergarten? Were there any fixed points in the weekly schedule? For example, did you visit your grandparents on Sunday, did you go to a sporting event on Saturday? If I think back to that time, what do I remember which was related to my mother?

1st Naikan question: What did my mother do for me in my preschool years? Maybe she prepared my food, can I remember what she cooked? Maybe she baked or organized something for my birthday or Christmas?

2nd Naikan question: What did I do for my mother in my preschool years? Maybe I made or painted something for her in arts and crafts for Mother's Day? Maybe she told me to put away my toys and I did it?

3rd Naikan question: What difficulties did I cause my mother in my preschool years? Did I make her worry? When I was sick or had hurt myself, when I came home too late from my friends?... Did I perhaps cause her to have more work? When I broke dishes through carelessness or clumsiness and she had to clean up the pieces, when I didn't want to eat something and she prepared another meal especially for me...

Did we just have different desires or interests? When I didn't want to go to bed at night and my mother had to go to work the next morning and I just wanted to keep playing... Did I intentionally cause a problem? When I deliberately looked for a fight...

It's NOT about who was right, it's also NOT about whether you were a good person or not. It's just about seeing how you behaved and what impact that had on the other person. Naikan doesn't judge. After you have worked through the pre-school years with Naikan, focusing on your mother, the next stage of life is examined, for example elementary school, 6-10 years. And so it goes on in time intervals of about 4 to 6 years, i.e. 10-14 years, 14-19 years... up until the present day.

Naikan with the focus on my mother — and then?

After focusing the 3 Naikan questions on your mother, your father usually follows. Thereafter, a person from your nuclear family is recommended, for example siblings or grandparents. During the week the focus will usually come back to your mother a second time.

Current relationships are considered in Naikan, e.g. your partner or your own children. Friends or colleagues, topics such as your career, lying and stealing, your body, health, etc. may be topics in Naikan.

Why my mother? I have no problem with her!

Well, all the better! If you have no problem with your mother (or another person you are focusing on in Naikan), then that's one more reason to enjoy the Naikan questions. Naikan also makes sense if the history with your mother (or another person you are focusing on in Naikan) has already been worked out. Because the Naikan questions and the chronological biographical work allow additional perspectives on other people and on yourself.

Working through your life story — without gaps

A person will always be examined from the first contact until now, or until such time as that person left your life. For parents and grandparents, you start the Naikan exercise from the time of birth, time period for time period, to date (or until that person died). For other people (partners, friends, colleagues…) you start from when you met them, chronologically until today, or until you lost contact.

You shouldn't leave out any stage of life, even if you sometimes didn't have a lot of contact. Each stage of life is included in reflection. After all, it's not about categorizing the events as "important" and "unimportant", but to see the many aspects of the relationship.

Recognize the past

A Naikan participant said the following after her Naikan week: "I thought that I would take a look at my past, work through it, and then push it away. But that doesn't work." That's the truth, you can't just push away the past, whether you have worked through it or not. Because every experience that we have made is stored in us and has an impact on our present lives. Naikan teaches us that we should integrate each experience and can build our future on this basis.

*How comfortable one is with people,
who treasure the freedom of others.*

Friedrich von Schiller

The Naikan conversation

During a Naikan week, the Naikan guide will come to you 8 to 10 times a day to have a short conversation with you at your Naikan place. This is how Naikan gets structure and you receive support during your exercise.

What a Naikan conversation is like

The Naikan guide will bow and ask, "Who are you focusing on and in what time frame?"

The Naikan participant then replies: "I am focusing on [the person concerned] from the time when I was [… to…] years old. What [the person] has done for me: [1 to 3 specific situations]. What I have done for [the person]: [1 to 3 specific situations]. What difficulties I have caused [the person]: [1 to 3 specific situations]."

The Naikan guide responds: "Please focus on [this person] and examine yourself in the next time period [for example the next 4 years]. Do you have another question?" [Responds if a question is asked] — "Thank you."

After the Naikan guide has thanked the participant, he or she bows again and goes to the next Naikan participant for a conversation. The Naikan conversation takes about 5 to 10 minutes.

Listening — without interpretation

Ideally, the conversation is very similar to the example just shown. No interpretations of what was said are carried out. We are not looking for explanations, or exploring causes, we are not forming connections. It is only about the facts, period. The Naikan guide only intervenes when the participant has difficulty working with the Naikan questions.

Which person or what subject and what period of time are considered next, is agreed upon in the Naikan conversation. The mother and father are always focused on in Naikan. The other people or topics are different depending on the person.

Just listening — nothing else?

A Naikan participant said the following at the end of a Naikan day: "Well, I can just as well tell my cat about it, she also won't say anything back." Yes, that is true. Because the task of the Naikan guide is to interfere as little as possible. However, there is a difference when listening: A person can really understand, a cat can't.

When does someone really listen to you? With open ears, an open heart and a keen mind? With appreciation and no urge to impose their own opinion upon you?

"There is something silent in every word, as a sign of where the word comes from — there is also something canting in every silence, as a sign that speech arises from silence."[11] Words originate from silence.

They give expression to what is unsaid. Naikan guides don't only hear the words, they also perceive, as well as they can, what is behind those words. They are not distracted by the words, they take that person as he or she is, at that moment.

Ishin Yoshimoto has the following instructions for the leading of Naikan: "Your main task is to listen to what the Naikan participant has to say. You must never believe that Naikan guides may conduct or direct or have an arrogant attitude. You always have to ask yourself: Am I balanced inside? Am I doing everything right?

Take very good care of yourself! You have an exact procedure to follow when guiding Naikan. Those who have come to Naikan did not come to listen to your chatter. Do you understand? Your task is only to listen. Do not chatter in between. If you interrupt the participant, how will he be able to find the thread again, which he lost because of you? After you have interrupted someone, you can't just say: 'Can you tell me again what you were about to say?' You are also not allowed to throw in a comment like, 'Yes, I understand that very well', and you're thinking: 'I'm itching, and I want to talk and talk, but I can't talk, this is a pain in the neck'. Yes, you need to control yourself. That's the most important thing as a Naikan guide, self-control."[12]

Do the other participants also listen?

If more than one person is practising Naikan in the same room, then the Naikan conversations are held in a whisper. This means that other people usually don't hear what is being said during the conversations of the other participants.

Sometimes there are conversations where someone whispers something a little louder — well, you don't have to purposefully listen. You are usually so engrossed in your own inner world that you don't really want to listen. Sometimes there is something that you overhear by chance, which may even be helpful to boost your own introspection.

Trust and appreciation

Self-reflection is a serious matter, no question about it. It is about comprehending your own sunny and shady sides, accepting them and finding a good way of handling them. Naikan guides usually listen with lowered eyes and a straight face. This is not a sign of a lack of interest, but expresses the deep respect for the participant.

And in addition to the very serious and salutary conversations, there is also shared laughter in Naikan. Because if humour forges ahead, then that means one thing above all: You no longer succeed in drifting amid the stream of feelings or thoughts, but you see yourself and other things from a different perspective.

During the Naikan retreat, trust between participant and guide grows, so that the shared laughter is also carried by mutual trust and appreciation, as emotional and serious moments are.

There must be hearts which know the depths of our being, and swear by us, even when the whole world forsakes us.

Karl Ferdinand Gutzkow

What are Naikan guides for?

As a Naikan guide, I serve the Naikan participant in the sense that he or she has the best conditions to practise Naikan. The accompaniment, with regard to the internal processes, plays the biggest role. Other important aspects, which Naikan guides are responsible for, are the organizational tasks.

Accompaniment during introspection

The primary task of Naikan guides is the accompaniment of each Naikan participant during the Naikan process. It is very difficult to put the importance of this function into words. If one were to compare the human world of experience, including all its positive and negative characteristics, to a mountain, then the Naikan guide would be the experienced mountain-climbing guide who has already explored the mountain in detail and therefore knows all the possible depths, formations and manifestations.

The Naikan participant comes with a sort of experience, with some forms of clear objectives with regard to this mountain, and looks for his or her own way to wander on this mountain. The Naikan guide accompanies the Naikan participant on his way, the guide will not push him in any direction or tell him where to go, neither will he or she tell the Naikan participants at which tempo they have to move.

As long as the participant moves with the help of the Naikan questions, nothing can happen, because the Naikan questions have the function of being the safety rope, with which you can safely move around the mountain. The Naikan guide will only intervene when the participant moves away from Naikan, in other words, when he throws away his safety rope.

The mountain remains the same in essence, but it is seen and experienced differently by each person. The mountain represents what is experienced by a human being in all its forms, such as joy, happiness, hope, faith, pain, grief, etc. These are always the same in nature, but are experienced divergently by every person in different contexts, situations and aspects.

Because every human being goes through these experiences in their own unique way, the Naikan guide is repeatedly able to learn to see new perspectives from the participants.

In the Naikan conversation the guide asks the Naikan participant where he or she currently is on their path. The Naikan guide also checks whether the participant continues to use his rope, namely the Naikan questions. If the guide makes suggestions or recommendations, then the Naikan participant always has the freedom to adopt and implement these, or not.

Respect, acceptance, trust

The Naikan guide respects the Naikan participant as he or she is. The guide respects the individual manner in which the participant goes about the Naikan practise. She accepts the Naikan process of the participant as it is. There are no educational or therapeutic targets that go beyond applying the Naikan method.

An essential task, when accompanying someone through Naikan, is to convey a sense of trust to the Naikan participant. As a Naikan guide I must have the ability to honestly trust that the experiences and perspectives of the participant are valuable, that he is capable of accepting things as they are, and that he can independently go his own way.

Listening and being silent

My job as a Naikan guide is to be the essence of calmness and to be able to listen attentively. My perception is fine-tuned: What is being formulated with words? What is resonating? Does something want to come out, which is perhaps hidden behind the words? The point is not to get distracted by the stories, but to perceive this person as a whole.

The first instruction to a Naikan guide is: Shut up! Because it is not my place to impose my opinion on the participant. So it is the most important task to just listen — with complete attention, with your entire mind, with all your heart.

I can only understand the other person by genuinely listening. My understanding is not brought across through my words, but through my silence. Understanding and being understood is a matter of feeling. Words often distract you from the essential, that is why Naikan places so much importance on silence and the scarce use of words. As a Naikan guide I constantly make sure that I choose my words carefully. Words and feelings should accord with one another. This makes a real dialogue possible.

Helping you through small and big crises

It sometimes happens that someone gets into emotional turmoil, is caught in a thought spiral, or other blockages arise, which the Naikan participant cannot free him or herself from. This is where the sensitivity of the Naikan guide is needed to provide assistance. In most cases, these small and big crises are resolved in a conversation, and sometimes there are other forms of assistance.

Competence and personal experience

A prerequisite for a Naikan guide to be able to accompany people in their Naikan processes, is to have extensive experience in their own personal Naikan process.

This primarily applies to dealing with the three Naikan questions, which one must have learned and practised.

Equally important is knowing one's own personal maturity, one's own behaviours, thoughts, feelings and everything else that makes up one's own being. I can only recognize in another person, what I have learned in my own experiences.

Therefore, the main basis for the existence as a Naikan guide, is one's own Naikan experience. To use the words of a good friend: "It is incredibly pretentious to believe that one can help anyone else with anything more than simply being there."

> Let us treat
> the sacred mystery of personality with
> respect; do not irreverently pelt in a man's
> inner sanctum.
> Thomas Carlyle

The bow

At the beginning and at the end of the conversation the Naikan guide bows to the Naikan participant. Bowing is a generally accepted form of respect in Japan and has therefore become a formal part in Naikan.

However, this is not merely a formality. The bow is an essential element of Naikan because the Naikan guide can express her appreciation for, and confidence in, the Naikan participant without using words.

I, as a Naikan guide, am not important, but rather the person who is practising Naikan. I serve the participant and am less of a guide than an accompanier. I listen and respect the insights of the participant without any interpretation of my own.

In addition, I bow to pull myself together and to prepare for the Naikan conversation. Because I want to be internally awake and alert for this person who is sharing his insights with me.

I bow to this person — not to his story, not to his ego, but to his internal being and his unique way of dealing with life's challenges. And to his ability to evolve and be a complete being.

Naikan participants sometimes ask me whether they should also bow. No, they do not have to. Of course, you are more than welcome to also bow if you feel the need to do so. It is simply an expression of appreciation.

Naikan participants often speak to me about the meaning and effect of the bow. A Naikan participant said that it repeatedly reminded him that it was about his own actions. He felt motivated anew, every time, and then thought: "Then I'll just do it."

*Treat yourself to yourself!
I am not saying: do this always.
But I am saying: do it once again.
Be there for yourself
as you are for everyone else.*

Bernard of Clairvaux

Remember, think, empathize

At first glance, Naikan may appear to be pretty top-heavy. You focus on a specific time period of your life and a particular person or topic, which you then analyse using three questions. So, training for the mind. That's one side of it. At second glance, it becomes clear that you examine your own experiences in Naikan. And we experience on all levels — with our head, heart, mind, emotions, body, soul.

The materials of the Naikan analysis are one's own complex experiences. It is logical that the full range of experiences come into perception when practising Naikan, including emotions. Feelings simply belong to one's internal experiences. However, the point is not to wallow in emotions or to get lost in thoughts. If this happens, the Naikan guide will be there to support you if you seem to be getting lost in the depths of your inner world.

Some people worry about whether they will recall sufficient memories. This concern is unfounded. It is not about the amount of memories, but about the devotion to oneself and the relevant stage of life. If memories come to mind then that is wonderful. If you can hardly remember anything at all then that is also okay. Because alone the willingness to deal with yourself and this phase of life, causes change and order in your inner life, albeit unconsciously.

Naikan is not a theoretical concept. It's something that we feel and experience directly. Our own experiences in our head, heart and mind are what make change possible.

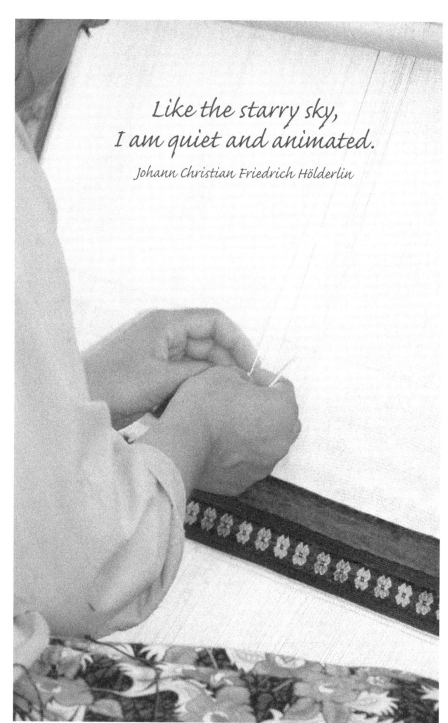

*Like the starry sky,
I am quiet and animated.*

Johann Christian Friedrich Hölderlin

The ups and downs of concentration

The idea of Naikan is continuous practise. In a retreat, this means trying to focus on Naikan every minute. You need to sleep and eat so you do have breaks. Because your body and mind have needs, we are sometimes distracted. However, you should constantly be focused on Naikan.

That's the theory.

In practise, it appears that you are able to concentrate more at certain times, and less at other times. Thoughts are distracting, feelings lead their own lives, the food tastes so good that nothing else matters... One wants to focus non-stop, but this is simply not possible.

I have never met anyone — I repeat — never met anyone who has been able to concentrate and focus on Naikan and their memory non-stop. If I do ever meet anyone who can do this then I'd be more worried than anything because I do not believe that sustained attention is possible.

The ups and downs of concentration are completely normal. Of course, the ability to concentrate increases when one practises. But it will always be subject to natural fluctuations.

Each participant receives a card with the 3 Naikan questions on it when attending one of my retreats, on which the following sentence is also written: "Please practise with all your power!" Many people interpret this as criticism and think that they are not practising "hard" enough. What does it mean to practise with all your power? I encourage everyone to ask themselves this question.

Practising with all your power sometimes means taking a break if fatigue sets in, or treating your body to a few relaxation exercises if you are tense. Naikan means introspection, it is not a mere technique of questioning. It is just as valuable as the Naikan work to be able to observe and respect the signals from the body and the internal life, here and now.

Writing in the book of life

Can I write something down? This question is probably one of the most asked questions. Is it allowed to write notes, make an entry in a diary or draw pictures? If it helps you to get in contact with the memories and your inner world, and if it helps you with regard to the Naikan questions, then by all means.

The basic rule when practising Naikan is: Anything that helps introspection and helps you to work with the Naikan questions is fine. If it distracts you from Naikan introspection, then you should leave it be. Practising Naikan should not turn into a writing exercise.

Every Naikan guide has a different opinion whether writing and drawing should be allowed during Naikan. In my personal opinion, I believe that you should just try it and see for yourself if it supports or distracts you.

There are some Naikan guides who clearly advise you not to write, or entirely prohibit it. Because writing often means that you are "working through" something.

Preparing and working through something is often targeted at a specific problem or solution, it serves a purpose, you want something "done". It's true that you work through knowledge and insights in Naikan. However, it is not about this part of working through something. It's about introspection, a meditative look into yourself. The point is to feel. It is not about feeding the mind. Just see what really is, for no particular reason, for no particular purpose. Let the images, feelings, insights, and knowledge emerge, let everything be, don't hold onto anything.

The book of life is written with what and how we live. We can sharpen our senses. Whether we put it on paper or not, is not the point.

Freedom of movement

Sitting for a whole week? No movement? Always sitting in a room? How can one handle that?

I very often hear that people who have an interest in attending a Naikan retreat could hardly imagine managing a week without nature or sports. A Naikan participant, who also had these thoughts, chose a Naikan venue where walks in nature were possible at any time — and she was surprised that she didn't want to leave her Naikan exercise place by the fifth day. She would have never expected that. Some stages of the inner work simply require the protection of the silent cocoon that you are offered.

If you know that you are a person who feels very restricted if you aren't able to go out into nature, then you should choose a Naikan venue where walks in the garden, or in the surrounding area, are possible.

If you do not wish to omit exercise for a week, then you should also choose a Naikan venue where you can jog outside or do other exercise. If it is less about nature and more about the possibility of having physical exercise in your daily routine, then a single Naikan room is the best choice for you. If you have the whole room to yourself then you have more freedom of movement.

The general recommendation in Naikan is to spend as much time on your practise place, but there is no prescribed posture. I like to say: You can sit, lie down, stand up, do a head stand… As long as it is helpful in focusing on Naikan it's wonderful. Experience has shown that an upright sitting position is best. Just try what suits you.

By the way, one week is not particularly long. Every person can easily adjust to a new routine for this time period.

Work meditation

Work meditation is not an integral part of the Naikan setting and is not practised at all the Naikan venues.

Where work meditation is practised, the participants are asked to perform a small task once a day. It is usually an activity in the home such as preparing vegetables for the food, vacuuming, cleaning the bathroom etc.

The participants are asked to continue with the Naikan questions during the 20-30 minutes of work meditation. This enables you to already practise Naikan in the retreat setting as you would when doing daily chores at home.

It is about carrying out an activity consciously and with tranquillity.

That is also why it is called "work meditation" and not "finish as quickly as possible". You can learn a different approach to work, which you are used to doing in everyday life. And many Naikan participants are able to use this attentive and pleasant way of working in their everyday life after the Naikan week.

By the way, work meditation is not a mandatory task, but rather a request. If you do not want to do it then that is also fine. One spends most of one's time sitting on the practise space and the movement during the work meditation is often experienced as a welcome change. Furthermore, many participants had unexpected Naikan insights during work meditation.

It is also nice to contribute to the community. The only task you have during a Naikan retreat is to dedicate your time to your own introspection. Everything else is taken care of. The desire to also contribute something often arises. This is where you can contribute, during work meditation.

The whole life of man is but a point of time; let us enjoy it, therefore, while it lasts, and not spend it to no purpose.

Plutarch

The delicious food

Many Naikan participants rave about the good food at Naikan. Why is something so ordinary seen as so extraordinary?

The daily routine in a Naikan retreat is quite simple and offers little variation. Therefore, meals are often perceived as a highlight. In addition, an appreciation for small and unspectacular everyday things arises in Naikan — like eating. What is hardly paid attention to in everyday life, is consciously taken note of in Naikan.

On the tray, which the Naikan guide brings to the participants, vegetarian food is usually served. Why is it vegetarian? Because the food should be easy to digest so that the body is well-fed, but not strained.

The supply of good food is an important aspect in order for the Naikan participants to feel good. Increasingly more people have food intolerances or allergies. If you inform the Naikan guide about this in advance then your needs will be taken into consideration.

Naikan means retreating into silence and reducing everything to the bare essentials. The following question therefore arises: Can I also fast during Naikan? Yes, you can. There are also offers for Naikan in combination with fasting. However, in your first week you shouldn't forego the food as you will appreciate the delicious meals as a power source for your internal work.

In his report about his Naikan week in Vienna, Mr. H. wrote: "The personally prepared meals by Ms. Schuh were delicious, well-balanced and allowed me to have a 'good gut feeling'." Of course, this was great to hear because praise is really nice. Many Naikan guides cook the meals themselves, or coordinate with the chef at the venue. It doesn't matter who cooks, I've always experienced that the great cuisine received amazing appreciation.

Can one attend a Naikan retreat more than once?

Yes, of course you can attend a Naikan retreat more than once. In business you take inventory once a year, in your home you spring clean annually, and in your inner workings you can also take inventory or spring clean once a year (or in other time intervals) by practising Naikan for one week.

After my first Naikan week I thought: Now I've done one week of Naikan, now I know it, that's enough for a lifetime. It only took half a year until I attended and practised at my second Naikan week. Today, a Naikan retreat is like meditation for me; Just observing, seeing my life path again, with no expectations and, surprisingly, I still recognize new connections and meanings.

Does one always start with one's mother?

Since a Naikan week begins by focusing on one's mother, I often hear the question, "Does one always start with one's mother?" Even if you are practising Naikan for the second, fourth, or tenth time?

Normally, yes. The Naikan exercise, with the focus being on your mother, is familiar, you don't have to find anything new and therefore you have no expectations, so it is a relaxed entry point to Naikan. However, you can start the Naikan week with another person if you wish.

Everything's fine

A Naikan retreat is like taking inventory of your own past. What key relationships were there in my life? What dynamics did these relationships have? The experience will be arranged and ordered through Naikan introspection, useless things will be sorted out, useful things will be valued, and unfinished business will be concluded. Whether you need one, two, or more Naikan weeks for this basic inventory of your inner life is different for each individual.

Eventually, you will have no more relationships to put in order, no more problems to solve, no unfinished business to conclude (which Naikan is, of course, excellent for). At some point your inner life will be just fine, you will have clarified your relationships, and have made peace with your past. There is nothing more to do. Nevertheless, you can continue to practise Naikan.

If you do Naikan just like that, without specific questions, without wanting to find a solution to anything, then you can draw from the depths of your inner life. If you are Naikan-trained, every person and every topic becomes a gate of perception. What has X done for me? What have I done for X? What difficulties have I caused X? Regardless of which person or what subject you consider, you will always find yourself in the interplay with the world.

In-depth Naikan

When you are proficient with the three Naikan questions and are able to order your own life history with regard to the core people in your life, then you can move onto other issues and topics.

One variant of in-depth Naikan is the topic of ethical conduct and behaviour. How was and is your behaviour with regard to ethics? Not only in theory, but based on what you have actually lived, done and experienced?

Your own experience causes a deep recognition that the quality of life increases by conducting yourself in an ethical manner.

Each Naikan retreat is different because the previous insights form a good foundation and your perspective now builds on that, or even goes beyond it. The experiences that have been made since the last retreat broaden the image of yourself and the world — if you look. The world is changing, you yourself are changing. It makes sense to observe this and to practise Naikan repeatedly.

Count Your Age by Friends, not by Years   *(John Lennon)*

Naikan experiential report by Ulrike R.

3 Naikan weeks for my family and friends...

I started to practise Naikan in Brazil one and a half years ago, at the age of 48. My motivation to do Naikan came from the same place that had caused me to do therapies and spiritual practises.

There was a latent dissatisfaction with my life. I was unable to match any of the parameters, which are common in today's society, that represent a successful life, and that at the age of almost 50 years. I didn't have a good professional position with a good income, I didn't even have a steady job, I hadn't started a family and didn't live in a solid relationship with a partner. I think, frankly, I had latent feelings of inferiority with regard to people who had these attributes, especially when they asked me why I didn't have what they had.

It was probably this troubled self-esteem that made me stay away from my family for more than 10 years. When I was there I heard questions and comments with the subtle requirement to meet those attributes and standards. I had lived in Brazil for 15 years and had only had very sporadic telephonic and written contact with my parents and siblings in the last 10 years.

I had also lost contact to the friends from my student days. Our life paths had separated, different topics had arisen, this also made me fall into a melancholic state. On the other side, my friendships in Brazil, from different stages of my stay, in various parts of the country far away from each other, were also without context.

The first Naikan week was a startling rediscovery of my past, using the 3 Naikan questions (1. What has the person done for me? 2. What have I done for this person? 3. What difficulties have I caused this person?). It was a very meaningful experience for me to remember and to perceive every detail of what my mother, my father, the community and my siblings did for me.

It was like, "I remembered myself." And I drove home feeling that I had had a really rich life. I just hadn't been able to perceive it before that.

I had the impression that I had always looked at the problems in previous therapies, and not at the good things in my life and the richness of relationships I had had. Based on this, difficulties, which I thought had been marked by my childhood, faded. I could perceive my parents as people who had taken on enormous difficulties to give me and my siblings the best life possible.

I immediately called my sister after the Naikan week and suddenly, to my surprise, there was such a relaxed atmosphere on the phone that we really laughed at ourselves. I was very touched by this and other "post Naikan events", that I made the decision, after 10 years, in spite of all the uncertainty of my personal situation — no fix job, no permanent residence — to visit my family and friends in Germany 6 months after my first Naikan retreat. I was still uncertain, the feeling of being a failure was apparently deep-seated. I asked myself, "How am I supposed to face them, I have nothing to show for myself?" And so I booked another Naikan week to start off my Germany trip. I was even picked up from the airport by the Naikan guide. My trip was beginning well.

In the 2nd Naikan week I had the opportunity to look at my life again, from a different Naikan perspective. Because this time I wasn't practising classic Naikan, but a themed Naikan for ethical conduct.

The emphasis was on the 3rd question, the difficulties, the topic of "lying and stealing" in its various forms, in relation to others and to myself. Through this part of Naikan I could see the motivations that were the basis for the decisions in my life. I had gotten used to seeing my life as a combination of a series of adverse conditions, unfulfilled desires and an attitude of "making the best out of situations." For example, I went to Brazil because I didn't have permanent employment in Germany — it was something like "taking the bull by the horns" and moving forward.

I could finally see, through Naikan, that there was a type of searching, and a commitment with clear justifications behind it all. I just didn't express this openly because it didn't encounter a positive response in my social circle. It has to do with honest work and true human relations, beyond securities and certainties of modern society. These desires led me to Brazil, where I met all kinds of people and experienced many projects and environments. It was hard for me to admit my limitations in finding a truer world. And it was even harder for me to realistically acknowledge how incapable I had been of communicating with my loved ones. Perhaps the one cannot be seen if it is isolated from the other, who knows?

I know that I only gained distinctive insights through clear observation of how I deal with the respective issues in my life. The biggest lie is omitting, not perceiving and not expressing so many aspects of reality — mostly those that were uncomfortable for my own desires. I also noticed that the judgments that I made about my own behaviour, at the beginning of the Naikan week, dissolved and disappeared. I think something similar happened with regard to my person in the 2nd Naikan to what I experienced in relation to my parents in the 1st Naikan week. What remains is understanding, or perhaps the willingness to simply listen…

I believe that Naikan gave me the clarity to see the people, who had been part of my life in Germany, in a particularly honest and open way, especially my mother. I was able to express my profound satisfaction and my joy at the wealth of our shared lives, and could, on this basis, address what had brought problems into the relationship from my point of view. I noticed how the superficial friendliness, which was typical of some of my relationships, made way for closeness.

I also believe that the decision that I made in the subsequent period, to spend six months in the AS ONE Community in Suzuka, Japan, was influenced by this Naikan week. Despite my efforts to express myself, there were still comments like: "Now you are almost 50 years old and still don't know where you belong, you have to make a decision now." But I can now look at this in a much more relaxed manner.

I found it interesting to learn that Naikan is a regular activity of many of the members in the AS ONE Community. Later, I was able to attend a local course there (with translation). The topics of these courses, as well as the relative "isolation" in everyday life due to my initial inability to communicate in Japanese, gave me another chance to look at my life from new Naikan perspectives.

Among other things, I discovered that I had developed a new type of lifestyle over the past 7 years, that enabled me to work on socio-ecological projects and live with my friends in Brazil, as well as with my recently reacquired friends and family in Germany. I was able to recognize this as a real priority in my life and take the step to go to Japan and meet the AS ONE Community, as a logical continuation of what I had already experienced.

In a conversation, which was initially about Naikan experiences, a person, who had lived in different communities in Japan for about 30 years, told me the following: "I also haven't earned any money in my life, but I have lived with many people and made many friends." And today the AS ONE Community sees itself as a "family of friends".

I think that I became happier and more satisfied with my past, and it has also allowed me to see my future path more clearly. It showed me who I really am, regardless of the current values of our society.

Practising Naikan for a whole week is a unique opportunity for me, without distraction, without external influences, to think about the topics of my life. To observe the reality of my relationships with my fellow human beings, and also the relationship with myself. This gives me security. The rhythm of my life has perhaps changed, has become a bit slower, to perceive more, to omit less, and to have real relationships.

The impression that I got from the AS ONE Community is that Naikan apparently helps to establish a very attentive environment between people, it also seems that the effect of Naikan completes and strengthens the other courses which are offered there.

I experienced my 3rd Naikan week in Japan. I again practised with the themes of traditional Naikan — mother, father, important relationships — in a somewhat modified version: To see myself in the personality-forming relationships, including the protect and escape mechanisms, which I developed there... and I was able to find more peace with regard to my father who passed away. I had the feeling that I was shedding layers of hardened skin and I was coming closer to what one could perhaps describe as 'human essence'.

I sometimes wonder what my life would have been like if I had come across Naikan earlier and started to practise 20 or 30 years earlier… I think my life would have been different, I think the people around me and I myself would have been happier and my life may have been easier. Therefore, I wish you all that you have the openness to experience Naikan at least once in your life, sooner rather than later.

Written in 2013, about three Naikan weeks in Brazil, Germany and Japan.

If we assume that one week of Naikan is like setting up a telegraph pole, then daily Naikan is the connecting wire.

Ishin Yoshimoto

4. Naikan — Can I do this alone in everyday life?

The Naikan technique, the 3 questions and the focus on a specific person or topic, works very well in your normal everyday life. This is an example of how you can incorporate Naikan into your everyday life:[13]

- Set specific time aside for Naikan (e.g. 15 minutes in the morning, 30 minutes in the evening, 1 hour on the weekend...).
- Combine an activity that you do regularly (e.g. ironing, the walk home from work, jogging...) with Naikan.
- Use short periods, which are unused or boring, for Naikan (waiting for the subway, travel times...).
- Keep a Naikan diary in which you write down your Naikan answers.

You should listen to your inner signals when you are practising alone. Don't expect anything in particular, don't look for anything special in the Naikan questions, just observe what comes up. You will notice that you automatically judge things as good or bad. This needs to be unlearnt, or more correctly, looked past. Whether it's pleasant or uncomfortable, it's healthy to be able to perceive all aspects.

The feedback from Mr. J., about a month after his Naikan week, shows that Naikan works well in everyday life: "I have learned to love day-Naikan. Both the individuals with whom you have contact during that day, and the day in general. You see the network which you are a part of more clearly, and the 'little things' like green leaves on the tree or sounds that the day has given you receive more appreciation and you are a lot more thankful."

Naikan throughout the day — simple and effective

Look back at your day in the evening, think about people with whom you had contact — in person, over the phone, via e-mail — and ask yourself:

1st Naikan question: Who did something for me today?
2nd Naikan question: Who did I do something for today?
3rd Naikan question: Who did I cause difficulties for today?

This is one of the easiest ways to practise Naikan every day. It only requires a few minutes of your time.

You can go through your day once more, in the evening on your way back from work or at home before bedtime.

You can also select a specific person with whom you had contact that day, and ask yourself the three Naikan questions:

1st Naikan question: What did this person do for me today?
2nd Naikan question: What did I do for this person today?
3rd Naikan question: What difficulties did I cause this person today?

Practising Naikan with regard to the day that passed, will help you to process the abundance of daily impressions and experiences and to sort them out. In this way you can leave the excitement of the day behind you and come to rest.

A Naikan participant gave me the following feedback on everyday Naikan: "I use the Naikan questions while lying in bed quite often, and I haven't made it to the third question thus far :-) I always fall asleep very deeply and happily before getting to it."

Naikan with the focus on a specific person

1st Naikan question: What has person X done for me?
2nd Naikan question: What have I done for person X?
3rd Naikan question: What difficulties have I caused person X?

If you want to focus on a specific person in everyday Naikan then you can proceed in two ways:

Option 1: Divide the time periods, from the first encounter with this person up to today, into sections. The sections can be a few years, months, weeks, days, depending on how long you have known the person. Concentrate on a different period every day, chronologically from the first time you met up to now.

This approach corresponds to classic Naikan, this is how you would practise it in a Naikan retreat. It provides a comprehensive view of the experiences that you have had with this person.

Option 2: Focus mainly on the most recent experiences. The last few days, weeks, months. You can focus on a different person every day. Or you can focus on the same period and the same person for several days in succession. It will be fascinating either way.

You can choose anyone from your private or professional life to focus on in Naikan. There doesn't have to be a special occasion to take a closer look at a relationship. Naikan can also be especially helpful if it is not going particularly well with someone. In case of conflicts, the Naikan questions can be used to perceive the person as a whole being again, and not to limit your perception to the current problem.

*We are made
for cooperation, like hands, like feet,
like the upper and lower jaws.*

Thomas Jefferson

Naikan with the focus on your partner

Has the daily-life in your relationship become boring or is it being taken for granted? Then it is high time to pay attention to your relationship:

1st Naikan question: What has my partner done for me in the past few weeks?
2nd Naikan question: What have I done for my partner?
3rd Naikan question: What difficulties have I caused my partner?

Look specifically for the small things, the everyday things — because the quality of a relationship is especially defined by the so-called little things.[14]

Have you recently argued with your partner? Then it is even more highly recommended to bring clarity to the emotional and mental confusion with the help of the three questions:

1st Naikan question: What has my partner done for me through this fight? What did he or she want to bring across or change?
2nd Naikan question: What have I done for my partner through this dispute? Was I able to listen? Was I able to bring my point across?
3rd Naikan question: What difficulties have I caused my partner? Was it necessary? Did I block something out? Was I careless?

Do not shy away from negative emotions — especially when someone hurts you, it is important to examine the situation very closely. You will see that it is precisely this "uncomfortable" feeling that makes Naikan infinitely valuable.

Naikan with the focus on a topic

When practising Naikan with the focus being on a specific topic, you perceive several different individuals who are associated with that topic.

It is advisable to ask the Naikan questions about all the persons who play a role:

1st Naikan question: Which people have done something for me with regard to [the topic]? Who, and what exactly?
2nd Naikan question: For whom have I done something with regard to [the topic]? For whom, and what exactly?
3rd Naikan question: What difficulties have I caused other people with regard to [the topic]? Who, and what exactly?

When answering each Naikan question, you consider which people play a role and what specifically comes to mind about these various people. If this seems too complicated or confusing to you, then you can always focus on an individual person with regard to the three Naikan questions, and do this with each person one after the other.

You can also ask the three Naikan questions with regard to the topic:

1st Naikan question: What have I gotten through [the topic per se]?
2nd Naikan question: What have I done for [the topic per se]?
3rd Naikan question: What difficulties have I caused [the topic per se]? Have I caused myself difficulties? (Also in the sense of: What could I look out for or improve on the next time?)

Think about whether all three questions really make sense. If your focus is on the topic of "my body", then all three questions fit: What has my body done for me? What have I done for my body? What difficulties have I caused my body? However, if you choose the topic "illness", then the question of "what difficulties have I caused my illness?" is of course nonsense.

Which topics can you choose for Naikan?

- General topics such as work, career, education, health, illness…

- Special topics such as a specific work meeting, a particular conflict situation, a family reunion, the working week, the current day…

Absolutely everything is suitable as a topic for Naikan. The important thing is always to remain specific and consider the three Naikan questions with regard to the people who are paramount in that context.

Here are some suggestions of what could be found on the topic of, for example, work:

1st Naikan question: a) What have people (boss, colleagues, customers…) done for me in relation to the topic (work)? For example, my colleague patiently explained a new work process to me. My superiors approved my desired vacation days. A customer thanked me for my kindness. My partner picked me up from my office so that we could go to a concert afterwards. When I asked him, a colleague gave me some advice in a difficult situation… b) What have I gotten through my work? For example, recognition, money, skills, contact with people…

2nd Naikan question: a) What have I done for other people (boss, colleagues, customers…) in relation to the topic (work)? For example, I completed a task for a colleague. I had a longer consultation with a customer. I made coffee for my colleague. I made a proposal to improve workflow in the office… b) What have I done for work? For example, be punctual, care, invest time, gain expertise, be patient…

3rd Naikan question: a) What difficulties have I caused other people (bosses, colleagues, customers…) in relation to the topic (work)? For example, I forgot to inform a colleague about a particular work process. I was having a bad day and lost patience with a customer. I came to work late and my colleague had to take care of my clients because of it. I told my colleague about a conflict in the office again, which then became too much for him… b) What could I be more aware of? For example, I get impatient when I work for too long without a break, so I want to think about how I can take my breaks in better-spaced time periods…

Some like it complex

Whether someone likes to practise Naikan with a specific topic in mind, depends, in my experience, on the type of person you are.

Some people thrive when they practise Naikan and focus on a specific topic, because they love to explore complex relationships and find different variations and formulations of the Naikan questions.

Others become rather irritated at the diversity and consider it to be too cluttered and confusing — they prefer clear and manageable structures and enjoy the classic Naikan questions with the focus on a particular person.

Being creative according to Naikan logic

Naikan always follows the same logic, by which you can adapt the Naikan questions depending on the topic.

The 1st Naikan question looks at what comes from the outside (from other people or external influences or the object of contemplation per se): What has… done for me? What have I received? The 2nd and 3rd Naikan questions examine your own contribution, your own part, that which comes from within. 2. What have I done for…? 3. What difficulties have I caused…?

Just ask yourself which formulations work with regard to a specific Naikan topic. Feel free to get creative!

Naikan in the here and now

This is how you can apply the Naikan questions to the current situation, and not only to experiences that have already happened:

1st Naikan question: Who is doing something for me right now? What am I receiving from other people or my environment right now?
2nd Naikan question: What am I doing for other people or my environment right now? What can I do and what do I want to do for other people or my environment right now?
3rd Naikan question: What difficulties am I creating right now?

Naikan primarily examines what you have already experienced. You have a lot of material to better see, understand, and be able to accept how you are.

If you already have some experience with the Naikan questions, then you can use this as mindful practise in the here and now.[15]

Naikan with the focus on the future

Can you also ask the Naikan questions about something in the future? Yes. However, there is a difference: Naikan is largely based on facts, and if you examine the past then you have material that is based on facts. The future, however, is precarious and one can only use a realistic estimate as a basis for Naikan.

If you want to prepare for something using the Naikan questions, then you first make a realistic estimation of what is to come.

For example, in preparation for a work meeting, you could as the following questions: what is the topic? What are the conditions and procedures like? Who is involved? What is my role? What would I like to contribute or enforce?

Then ask the Naikan questions: According to my estimation…

1st Naikan question: Who and what is going to support me in this matter? In what way can I count on support? Who is expectedly going to do something for me, and in what way?
2nd Naikan question: What can I do to implement this matter? Who can I ask for assistance? How can I prepare?
3rd Naikan question: What difficulties do I see arising? Will I cause someone difficulties through this matter?

Things always happen differently than you expect, but preparation can be very helpful.

Naikan annual review and outlook

The Naikan annual review:

1st Naikan question: What have I received in the past year? Which people did something for me?
2nd Naikan question: What have I given in the past year? What have I done for other people?
3rd Naikan question: Which people have I caused difficulties for in the past year?

The Naikan outlook for the following year:

1st Naikan question: Which people will be in my life in the coming year? Who will most likely continue to support me, what can I continue to count on?
2nd Naikan question: What do I want to give in the coming year? Who do I want to do something for? What do I want to do for myself?
3rd Naikan question: Which people will I probably cause difficulties for? Can I alleviate these difficulties? If so, how?

Naikan biography work

You want to work similarly to a Naikan retreat and explore your life systematically?

Then do it like this:

• You should reserve at least 30 minutes per day for Naikan biography work because it takes some time to recollect the distant past. In addition, findings cannot be forced, but rather show up on their own if time and space is provided.

• Biography work needs a protected environment. It is helpful to not undertake your Naikan considerations on the way home or when listening to music, but to retreat to a quiet place to do so.

• Begin by focusing on your mother. On day 1 you explore your memories with the 3 Naikan questions in your pre-school years, that is when you were 0-6 years old. On day 2 you explore experiences from the age of 6-10 years old, 10-14 years on the 3rd day, and so on until today. Time periods of 4 to 6 years are recommended. If your mother is no longer alive, then your Naikan observation ends on the day of your mother's passing. Please select the person who took on the mother role if you did not grow up with your birth-mother.

• Always ask all three Naikan questions. Always ask the same three Naikan questions for each time period in which you remember your mother. 1. What did my mother do for me? 2. What did I do for my mother? 3. What difficulties did I cause my mother? You can, for example, allow yourself 10 minutes for the 1st Naikan question, the next 10 minutes for the 2nd question, and the last 10 minutes for the 3rd Naikan question. Write the answers down in your Naikan diary.

• Go through your life story relating to your mother from start to finish. Only then do you go onto the next person. It is very important, in Naikan biography work, to always chronologically consider a person from the first contact up until the present. Even if memories sometimes wander off to other people, the focus remains on the same person.

- You focus on your father as the second person in Naikan. Proceed just as you did when you were focusing on your mother.

- Thereafter, you select a person from your nuclear family. For example, grandfather, grandmother, brother, sister. Preferably someone who was close to you and with whom you had a lot of contact.

- Then we recommend that you focus on your mother once again. Firstly, you have now created an easier access point to your memories. Secondly, you will learn that you gain new perspectives if you observe something more than once. This is comparable to a work of art: You can observe a picture, a sculpture, a movie, time and again, and it will be inspiring every time.

- Which person from your family of origin would you still like to focus on? You can choose from your grandmother, grandfather, sister, brother, uncle, aunt, etc… You can look at as many people in succession as you like.

- Now choose your partner or a person from your current family. The first choice is your current relationship, so significant other, partner or spouse. You can also select other members of your current family for Naikan, for example, your son, daughter, grandchild, partners of your own children, in-laws…

- Now you have done basic biography work. Of course, you can continue with Naikan from here on. Any person or topic is suitable for Naikan. You can focus on people who you have already focused on with Naikan a second time, or even more often.

- If you want to complete your biography work, then we recommend Naikan to do so. Look back at the period in which you practised Naikan. 1st Naikan question: What have I gained through the biography work with Naikan? 2nd Naikan question: What did I do for the Naikan biography work? 3rd Naikan question: What difficulties have I caused in connection to the Naikan biography work?

- Naikan biography work requires about three months of daily practise.

If you require support during Naikan then contact a Naikan centre or a Naikan guide.

Naikan Diary

Date: ....

I practise Naikan about: ....

in this period of time: ....

1ˢᵗ Naikan question: What has .... done for me?

2ⁿᵈ Naikan question: What have I done for .... ?

3ʳᵈ Naikan question: What difficulties have I caused .... ?

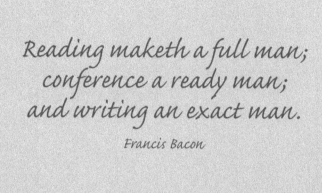

*Reading maketh a full man;
conference a ready man;
and writing an exact man.*

Francis Bacon

Written Naikan

If you practise every-day Naikan then it may be useful to write your Naikan answers in a diary. You can buy a diary, in which you make your notes, or make your entries in a computer.

What is a Naikan diary for?

It motivates you to practise Naikan. We often lose our interests in the hustle and bustle of everyday life. The Naikan diary helps you to remember the Naikan practise and allows you to stay on it.

Writing sometimes causes thoughts to become more clear because you have to formulate them. Valuable insights come to some people through writing.

Does one have to write down the Naikan findings?

No, of course not. The most important thing in Naikan is DOING. Valuable time is every single minute that you devote to self-reflection. It is irrelevant whether you write it down or tell someone about it.

Observe what type of person you are. If writing feels rather annoying and distracts you from the actual Naikan exercise, then avoid writing things down. If you find writing to be helpful, then a Naikan diary is a fine thing.

If you practise Naikan for a longer period, then your Naikan diary can show you the findings and changes that have come up. As a kind of afterthought.

5. Naikan — Why should I do it?

What type of people come to Naikan? What motivates them to retreat for a week and intensively think about themselves?

The motives are very different for each person. There is often a specific reason, a current issue or a problem that one would like to clarify. This could be a familial or a professional issue, or inner confusion. Sometimes it is a current difficulty and sometimes it is a lifelong issue that calls for a further step towards clarity.

More and more people are drawn to a Naikan retreat by their desire for a break. They want to get away from the hubbub of everyday life, from the constant commitment, they want to find inner peace, have time for themselves. And they use this time to take care of their internal self.

I hear the following statement all too often: "I don't need Naikan, I don't have a problem." Then I say: "Well, that is even better." Because Naikan was not created to solve problems, but rather as a tool to explore yourself. So if you are simply curious about yourself and your life, then Naikan is a good choice.

To better understand yourself is a common reason to practise Naikan. It is sometimes also about recognizing a purpose in your life. Naikan doesn't convey ideologies, and therefore offers a lot of space for you to find your own answers to the spiritual question of the meaning of life.

I also hear: "I don't need Naikan… But I know someone who it would be really good for." Believe me, it doesn't really work to not have done Naikan yourself and want to bring someone else to Naikan. Rather try Naikan yourself. Others will only be inspired to try Naikan if they have seen that you have done well with it.

I want to find peace and recharge my batteries

In everyday life, with its enormous demands, there never seems to be enough time to really take care of yourself. Faster, better, more — that is the motto, both in professional and private life. More and more power is required, regardless of the cost of personal resources used up. A reinforced need for a break arises from this. Find peace, regain strength — one can also do that on vacation. If you wish to go beyond that, to look at the way you live, to observe the way you deal with yourself and others, then Naikan is a good choice for you. Because Naikan combines time off with the care of one's own inner life.

Finding inner peace means getting through to yourself. Getting through to yourself means being in contact with yourself. One Naikan participant said, "Well, then I just speak to myself." It's about inner dialogue, regardless of whether it happens consciously or unconsciously, whether you experience it like an inner conversation or whether simple thoughts and feelings are perceived, which have no place in everyday life.

Regaining strength means feeling your internal resources again.[16] Inner strength is fed by your experiences, and how you deal with those experiences. Therefore, in Naikan, you examine what you have experienced, you take inventory of your inner life. It's about gaining insight into the way in which you have organized your life, and how you wish to shape it further. By the way, knowledge is not limited to the processing of childhood events, but is possible at any age, with any person or any topic.

You will emerge internally strengthened after Naikan, because by looking at what you have lived through, you see more clearly how you plan to use your strength from now on. And the peace of the time-out has a lasting effect.

*If I were two-faced,
would I be wearing this one?*

Abraham Lincoln

I'm curious — self-awareness

How do I tick? According to what pattern do I function? Why does something happen to me over and over again? How do I make clear decisions? Can I take care of myself better? What am I still capable of? How can I live more consciously? These are questions that people ask, who are just curious about themselves and want to get to know themselves better.

Self-awareness is a conscious process, because, as the name suggests, you want to become more aware of something about yourself. It is about perceiving your own thought patterns, behaviours, feelings, needs, skills, prejudices, values, and so on... Who am I? What can I, or do I want to, learn or change? The more I know about myself, the clearer my individual development opportunities become.

Recognize and know yourself — but how?

You become most aware of yourself if you have an opposite to go on. The perception of "I" and "you" is part of self-awareness; So is the ability to distinguish between who does what? In order to train this perception there is the technique of the three questions in Naikan: 1. What has person X done for me? 2. What have I done for X? 3. What difficulties have I caused X?

The best way to find something out about yourself is to look at how you have lived up to now. That's why Naikan works with one's own biography, you see yourself in your own course of life, in light of your own experiences. And the three Naikan questions allow new perspectives to be recognized.

Getting to know yourself is a lifelong process. Anything that is learnt and recognized through your own experiences is more powerful than what is conveyed from the outside. Naikan, as a method of self-awareness, creates access to your own experiences, to your own power, and to yourself.

I am suffering — self-healing and self-help

How can I solve my problems? How can I fix my relationships? How do I get over separation and loss? How can I deal with anxiety or illness? How can I cope with painful experiences? I'm in a crisis, how do I get out? Why does something happen to me over and over again, what am I doing wrong? This is a small selection of the questions people ask when they have problems and can't cope with something in their lives.

Most people who come to Naikan have a specific reason, an issue, a problem. There is something that they want to solve, something that they want to overcome. The desire for happiness and well-being is at the forefront.

The great gift of Naikan is that one's life can be experienced in a much greater setting than the reduction to a problem or a disease. In Naikan, you consider yourself, your entire life, and even people who may have nothing to do with your problem. Therefore, problems often lose their power.

Of course you can also specifically deal with a problem in Naikan. Naikan is not therapy, so it can only open up additional perspectives on an issue. And that can be very helpful.

Yes, solutions for some problems do also arise in Naikan. There is much room for clarification and new perspectives in the silence of a retreat and in the structure of Naikan work.

New possibilities often show themselves when your view of the greater whole becomes clear.

Naikan is not a panacea. Psychological or psychosomatic problems have complex causes and fall within the spectrum of psychotherapy or medicine. Naikan is well suited as a supplement to psychotherapy or coaching.

I am looking — self-realization and spirituality

Where is my place in the world? Does my life have a purpose? How can I live what is in me? What is my role in this life? How do I find myself? How can I realize my potential? Who am I? Where does my spirit go to when I die? Such questions arise from people who are looking for the meaning of life.

Peace and happiness are the big topics when it comes to self-realization and spirituality. Spiritual matters are beyond one's own "little" happiness. The focus shifts to how to be involved as an individual in the community and in the world. Man is part of a larger whole. Every person has the inherent opportunity to find peace and fulfilment in themselves. The road to peace and fulfilment runs via self-development and self-realization. One method of self-realization is Naikan.

Some people have already found their faith, be it a religion or a spiritual path.

If you have already found your worldview then Naikan can be a good addition to this.[17] Because Naikan creates a direct link between your religion, your spirituality and your own life.

Plunge deeply into your being — that is Naikan. This experience of self is completely independent of what beliefs you hold.

Naikan cannot and does not wish to offer you a worldview, Naikan is not inherent to any religion. No wisdom teacher tells you what you have to believe or what you have to do. If you are looking for spiritual answers, then there is only one person who can give you these. That person is you.

Can anyone practise Naikan?

Yes, anyone can practise Naikan, regardless of age, if one feels the willingness to do so in oneself. My youngest Naikan participant was 14 years old, my oldest Naikan participant was 77. The age group between 25 and 65 is the most common in Naikan.

The only requirement for Naikan is the ability to distinguish memory and reality from fantasy and fiction. Thus, Naikan is not suitable for people with cognitive disorders, psychosis, or dementia. Caution is advised when using illegal substances and taking psychoactive effective drugs.

Naikan is a method of self-realization and is not a substitute for medical or psychological care.

In any event, you are required to have clear perception. In case of health limitations, please conduct a preliminary talk with the seminar guide. Taking medication or other substances which bring about a deterioration in perception and concentration, as well as other physical or mental limitations that require special consideration, are seen as health restrictions.

If you are in psychotherapeutic treatment, you should discuss with your therapist which time would be appropriate for a Naikan retreat.

Naikan requires your interest and participation. A Naikan seminar is not entertainment, you actively explore your own being. No teaching from the outside, but rather recognition from the inside. Therefore, Naikan works best when someone attends a Naikan retreat voluntarily. Naikan cannot be "prescribed", it can only be recommended. Someone who is obliged to practise Naikan will hardly be able to benefit from it. If you're interested and willing to deal with your inner world, then Naikan can unfold it's effects.

*The secret to happiness
is freedom.
The secret to freedom
is courage.*

Pericles

6. Naikan — What does it do for me?

As unique as human beings are, as unique is their feedback about their Naikan experiences.[18] Regardless of what people find in introspection, Naikan always brings personal development — self-determined, deep, lasting.

Many participants say: "I feel blessed, I feel rich." Because Naikan draws attention to what is there, to the richness of your own experiences. Problems lose power, potentials come to the fore.

The 1st Naikan question shows what you have received. Through the 2nd and 3rd Naikan questions you can see that you have been able to do something. Sometimes something goes wrong, but you have the ability to actively shape things.

The perspective rotates by 180 degrees. Usually, we find ourselves very important and our successes are attributed to our own strength, nothing seems to exist except for our problems. This selfish view undergoes a reversal through practising Naikan, because you notice how many people and things were a part of your own well-being and have contributed to your own development. I would not be able to live if other people and the world were not here for me. My being as a human is embedded in the universe.

Moreover, Naikan draws attention to the little things. We take so much for granted. You will suddenly perceive so much more through Naikan. One begins to perceive diversity, not only either this or that... but both this and that... Subsequently you live more mindfully and attentively, perhaps even more gratefully.

In any case, you go into dialogue with yourself, you find that there is more to you than meets the eye. Or as a participant said at the end of her Naikan week, "I feel as if I've found home after a long journey."

Self-realization, self-confidence, self-acceptance

Through the structured consideration of the past in the Naikan week, new prospects are added to one's own self. Memories are neither erased nor rewritten. The perspective of what we have actually experienced is simply broadened easily.

The comprehensive experience of the remembered situation is kind of unravelled: facts are distinguished from expectations, desires, feelings, thoughts, interpretations…

This creates a new, more realistic self-image that is no longer limited to those few events in the past that we have assessed as particularly memorable. A variety of perspectives are added to what you have experienced. "I'm always amazed at how my views have changed and how much I've started to love myself." This statement, from a Naikan participant some months after her Naikan week, shows how one's self-image can sustainably change. A new awareness of your own social behaviour arises. Because if you repeatedly check your own behaviour with regard to different people, you not only recognize your own patterns better, you also get a keener eye for the other persons reactions.

Mr. H. wrote the following in his experiential report: "The internal changes are sorting themselves out, a lot has moved in me. Firstly positively, but there are also many situations that I am now aware of. Where I want to go beyond my limits, or in the past actually did so. Or situations in which I was not myself and where I didn't act or communicate as I usually would have. The external reactions — be it from family members, friends and acquaintances — are positive. I realize how many people are touched by my personal journey. They feel it when I behave consistently with my inner being."

We are the image
which we paint of ourselves. We change.
Be careful that the image is not fixed.

Luigi Pirandello

Overcoming the past

If there are still unresolved issues in your own life story, then Naikan is a great way to make peace with the past. The structured involvement with one's own past in Naikan serves the purpose of accepting the past as it is.

Working with your memory is not meant to be a "relapse", even if painful feelings come back into consciousness. The 'I' of today remembers the 'I' of the past, the present 'I' ensures that one doesn't lose oneself in the past. In addition, the three Naikan questions offer support and orientation.

Experiences, which are unprocessed, often unexpectedly and undetectably mix into our present state. It is therefore beneficial if the following insight arises: Yes, parts of the past are painful, but there are also things that were okay, even enjoyable.

The most important step is the acceptance of what took place. We cannot change it anymore, that's just the way it was. As a Naikan accompanier, I have been able to experience acceptance of, and reconciliation with, the past many times — be it with a person or a specific event. This acceptance is so liberating.

One of the most touching moments for me is when a Naikan participant says, "It's actually amazing how I dealt with it." In moments like that the person doesn't just see, feel and accept what he has experienced, but he gives himself recognition for having been able to handle that situation. The human being is a wonderful creature: He seldom breaks under difficult circumstances, he usually grows because of them.

Through the recognition of all that has shaped your own life, you can let go of the past — because you are allowed to decide how you deal with your own life experiences.

New perspectives and new opportunities

"Naikan managed to show me, in just two days, that I can help myself and do not permanently have to bother other people with my abundance of feelings." Well, it doesn't always go as quickly as Waltraut F. mentioned in her report. But the fact is that you can see new opportunities and ideas emerge, with regard to how to better deal with situations, through Naikan.

One question does arise here: How are you supposed to get ideas for the future if you are always examining the past in Naikan?

The answer is simple. It is precisely because you are taking a close look at what has happened thus far, that you can clearly recognize the target for change, or corrections to your path.

Naikan increasingly directs our attention to our own part, to what we ourselves contributed to a situation. It shows that you can actively influence the way in which you look at something.

Sometimes Naikan participants utilize the inner clarity and calmness in the latter part of the Naikan week to focus on the future. Concrete ideas for change can occur in this way — no theories, but possibilities for everyday use that have been tailored to your own personality.

And if the view is no longer constrained by the demands of everyday life, then a larger perspective can become conscious: The orientation of one's own path in life. A Naikan participant wrote the following to me a few weeks after her Naikan week: "Naikan, or this retreat week, has had quite a profound and lasting effect on me. It's a feeling of having taken the thread of life into my own hands again."

Mindfulness and inner peace

"The miracle of life opens up anew to me each day." This is how David G. described how the three Naikan questions affect his actions in his daily life. I find it a beautiful way to describe how Naikan can enrich one's life as a mindfulness practise.

In everyday life, inner peace comes from the pause and the clarity of the Naikan questions. Because if it's clear what is going on, then one cannot easily be fazed.

In a Naikan retreat inner peace is created by the careful contact, the external silence and the growing inner acceptance of what one has experienced. The Naikan guide supports peace through his or her respectful and mindful behaviour.

The tools for internal work are the three Naikan questions and the interpersonal encounters, i.e. how we deal with one another. In Naikan it is less about who or what we are observing, and more about how we are observing the events. The content, so the situation in question, ensures that we inwardly take a step back and are able to take on the Naikan perspective. You do not let yourself be held captive by the situation or your own patterns, but, through the three Naikan questions, become aware of who has contributed what to a situation. Despite all the clarity you stay in touch with yourself, you remain mindful of yourself and other people.

Naikan is mainly the way in which you perceive, how you deal with your own consciousness.[19] Life remains as it is — colourful, varied and unpredictable. Naikan helps you to deal with what life throws at you in a more conscious and diligent manner.

Living in peace —
with myself, everybody and everything

We live in an affluent society and are influenced by the attitude of, "I deserve it, it belongs to me." We want everything cheaper, faster, better and exactly how we want it. We look at the world from this selfish perspective and mainly see what we don't have or what we want to change. And already you're in conflict with the world and usually also with yourself. So we long for peace.

But the truth is, "You don't deserve anything, nothing belongs to you." On the contrary, it is the role as a human in this existence, to lead your own life and fulfil your task as a human being. No more and no less.

It is natural that every human being is part of this world. Every person has — like any other being too — their place in the world, which is nothing special. Every individual is embedded in the whole.

It becomes visible, through Naikan, how other people and the world have helped you go your own way. And yes, you yourself have also done a lot for it. You will soon realize that you are living because many other people were there for you. You are living because many people and the world are there for you, even if they do not always perfectly match your own desires. This experience of being part of nature and the connectedness with everything, is accompanied by deep inner peace.

People often make deep experiences of 'being' in Naikan. Appreciation, deep feelings, connectedness, a clear awareness of the effects of each action, trees that seem to light up... As a Naikan guide I am always surprised at how many different forms of expression such an experience may have, and I am grateful that so many people share these with me. These experiences are rather unusual, but unspectacular. They open up a window to a larger dimension and are accompanied by a feeling of infinite calmness and peace. This awareness of inner peace continues to work in your everyday life.

Lead each thing back to its origin and observe wherein and whereby it degenerated, but at the same time consult both what the best of the past time was, and what the most suitable of the most recent time was.

Sir Francis Bacon

7. Naikan — Where does it come from?

The Naikan method was developed by a Japanese man called Ishin Yoshimoto...

That is how most descriptions of Naikan begin. You may think, "Aha, another self-proclaimed individual, who has found some type of salvation for humanity." Wouldn't the representatives of the Naikan method be better off not emphasizing the Japanese origin and its founder? Could they not — on a strictly scientific basis, of course — offer a sober description of the flow, content and target of Naikan?

The historical background of a method forms the basis of its understanding. Therefore, I think it is important to openly explain the history and the character of the founder of the Naikan method. A reputable method is also characterized by openness and transparency.

Naikan originated in the Japanese Buddhist-dominated culture.[20] The Naikan founder, Ishin Yoshimoto, was both a successful businessman and a deeply religious individual. Both aspects of his personality formed the foundation for the Naikan method. It is thanks to Yoshimoto's aspirations that Naikan is a method that has a broad action spectrum and can be practised regardless of religious beliefs.

By the way, Mr. Yoshimoto always rejected naming it "Yoshimoto-Naikan", or being dubbed as the Naikan founder. He said, "Buddha and Shinran are the founders of Naikan, I'm just the one who beats the drum." Moreover, the person who is practising Naikan is always in the foreground.

After a Naikan week Mr. Yoshimoto asked each Naikan participant what could be improved with regard to Naikan, and he implemented many of these proposals. Naikan guides are not masters, but servants of the people.

Founder of Naikan
Ishin Yoshimoto (1916-1988) and
his wife Kinuko Yoshimoto (1920-2000)

© Photo: Johanna Schuh

How Naikan became a method

Ishin Yoshimoto was born in 1916, lived in Japan, and died in 1988 at the age of 72. Initially, he worked as a salesman and eventually began an apprenticeship in leather processing. He slowly worked his way up to being the owner of a thriving business producing artificial leather products. He was very successful as a businessman and made millions in revenue.

Mr. Yoshimoto simultaneously studied calligraphy, an eastern art of writing. He practised this art throughout his life and his calligraphy pieces are still seen as high quality works of art. His Naikan calligraphy (illustration on page 251) is used, for example, in the Naikan logos in Europe and the US.

The spiritual background

As a devout Buddhist of the Jodo-Shin-School, Ishin Yoshimoto found many teachers and underwent various Buddhist exercises on his spiritual path. A strict Buddhist practise, which he practised several times, was Mishirabe.

Mishirabe required you, under the supervision of a Buddhist lay-priest or an experienced believer, to retreat into seclusion. One was shielded from external stimuli, was alone in a room, without food, water and sleep. The task was to ask the question, "Where do I go after death?", and one sought situations in one's life, in which one experienced love. The point of this exercise was to gain "real trust" in accordance with Jodo Shin Buddhism. So it was about having a very personal experience of deep faith besides the intellectual knowledge of religion and faith. Ishin Yoshimoto said: "It is not enough to know that fire is hot. You have to experience it yourself."[21]

After Mr. Yoshimoto had gained real trust, after several attempts in the Mishirabe exercise, on the 12th of November 1937, a deep need to find a practical method that was feasible for all people arose in him. Deep spiritual experiences should be able to be felt without subjecting the body to severe deprivation or to be linked to a religion. And it should be a method that can serve as a constant in one's life, so that deep, lasting effects and insights can be experienced in everyday life.

The economic background

In developing the Naikan method, the Naikan founders drew on his experience as a successful businessman. In business, you keep records of income and expenditure to check whether the balance is equalized. To reach a spiritual experience, you have to face death. This also means to take stock of one's life. So he placed the principle of accounting and taking stock onto social relationships: What have I received from a specific person, what has that person done for me? What have I given back to him? That is how the first two Naikan questions came to be.

An audit is carried out in clearly defined time periods. This structured approach also found its place in the Naikan method. At the beginning of Naikan, the focus is on the primary caregiver — this is usually the mother — in chronological periods of one's own life story. Thereafter, one examines oneself and other persons of interest in reasonable time periods.

Initially, there was no particular framework, the exercises took place parallel to everyday life.

Completion of the Naikan method

The Naikan practise only consisted of two questions for many years. It is not known how Mr. Yoshimoto developed the third Naikan question. Maybe it also originated from a business perspective, because you also check which vulnerabilities and disturbances are present in a company. This is where the question could be deduced from: What difficulties have I caused a particular person?

Another theory is that the development of the third Naikan question also goes back to the Buddhist roots. In Shin Buddhism one has to face hell in one's own soul, and the more the ego is ashamed, the sooner it steps aside and lets the "other force" come through.[22] Yoshimoto added a third question to the two original questions: What difficulties have I caused the person who I am focusing on?

Propagation of Naikan

Initially, Mr. Yoshimoto practised Naikan with his employees. Before 1945, he visited the surrounding villages and tried to encourage people to practise introspection. Naikan spread in Japanese prisons from 1955.

Thereafter, Ishin Yoshimoto opened a Naikan centre, which he led with his wife Kinuko. Naikan was offered there as a period of seclusion, as a retreat into silence from everyday life. The length of the retreat varied at the beginning, it only took on the form that it has today in 1968. Since then, a Naikan retreat has a length of seven nights. Mr. Yoshimoto recommended learning the Naikan technique during the first Naikan retreat, then practising Naikan daily, and repeating a retreat to refresh your knowledge from time to time.

In the early 1970s more Naikan centres originated in Japan, in the late 1970s Naikan came to Europe. The first Naikan centres emerged in German-speaking countries in the mid-1980s. It is thanks to Prof. Akira Ishii, professor of criminal law at the Aoyama Gakuin University in Tokyo, that Naikan is known in many countries of the world.

The Buddhist roots

Buddhism in Japan is primarily associated with Zen, because Zen Buddhism is well known here in Europe. However, the origin of Naikan has nothing to do with Zen. Ishin Yoshimoto developed Naikan based on the spiritual approach of Jodo-Shin-Buddhism.

Jodo Shinshu i.e. "The True School of the Pure Land," is one of the largest schools of Buddhism in Japan today. It dates back to Shinran (1173-1263). The main point of Shinran is the distinction between the two forces Jiri- Ki, one's own strength, and Tari-Ki, the other strength. While Zen emphasizes one's "own strength", so, awakening one's own power, Jodo-Shin emphasizes the "other strength". This means that the strength, which Amida-Buddha makes available to all beings out of compassion, leads to inner liberation. The assistance provided by the "other strength" is a gift and cannot be called forth by one's "own strength". This force begins to act spontaneously where there is faith and trust.

The concept of trust in the "other strength" plays an essential role in Naikan. It's not about the strict practise, but about the trust and dedication to the practise. One can prepare the ground through Naikan, but it is unpredictable when the seed of insight will be absorbed.

Insight cannot be forced by anything, it simply appears. Therefore, Naikan guides follow the concept of humility and service, so that the participant's process of realization can go forth largely undisturbed.

Although Mr. Yoshimoto found deep insight through the ascetic Mishirabe practise, he chose a middle way for Naikan: Retreat into silence with pleasant conditions, as much support as necessary and as little distraction as possible. Naikan should be feasible for all people and be manageable without religion or belief system. It is a method on how to clarify and expand your view of yourself and the world.

*Do Naikan
as an engagement with death.*
Ishin Yoshimoto

The big question of life and death

If you were to die right now, where would you go to?
For what purpose were human beings born?

Ishin Yoshimoto encouraged Naikan participants to ask such questions.[23] For him, the question of life and death was the essence of Naikan. In his eyes, the participant was finding his way to spiritual awakening through Buddha, which deserves deep respect. There are hardly any Naikan guides who ask questions about life and death today.

It is not easy to address death in a time when the thought of death is suppressed, and problems are fixed as quickly and as easily as possible. The temptation is also strong to reduce the Naikan method to self-discovery with therapeutic effects, or to reduce the three Naikan questions to a coaching technique. As valuable as self-awareness, therapy and coaching are, Naikan has a further dimension: The direct experience of being, that what we call spiritual experience.

A pause in the flow of time

"Looking at the past up to the present through someone else's eyes, stopping the time of life, that is Naikan."[24] Professor Akira Ishii speaks of Naikan as "a stop in the flow of time" because you pause to consciously observe yourself and what you have already experienced. You see yourself and your own life from a different perspective to how you would in daily life.

People who report near-death experiences describe a kind of life review, which makes life appear in a clear light. Why wait for death before reviewing your life? There is nothing that you can change then. It would be better to introspect in this life, so that you still have time to recognize the opportunities and turn your life in a wholesome direction.

Seeing the flow of life and yourself

A life review takes place in Naikan, in which a change of perspective takes place sooner or later.

In a lecture, Prof. Ishii held his hand out about twenty centimetres in front of his face and said, "I usually look from the inside at the outside world. While doing so I say: That's me! When I say that, then I see the inner surface of my hand. You, the people out there, also see my hand, but you see the back of my hand. We are both looking at my hand, but we see different things. Naikan is a method that allows me to see the back of my hand. I try to see myself how you see me from the outside." As a result, you get a clear picture and a clear sense of both the internal and the external, of the I and the you.

Once you are aware of the view that others have, another change of perspective takes place. Suddenly, you are no longer rowing on the middle of the river of life and looking at everything from this perspective, but you are now looking at yourself from the shoreline or from a bird's eye view.

When someone is attending a Naikan week for the first time, the introspection only gets this quality on the fifth day at the earliest. It is never predictable when such moments of insight arise.

It is a change to a different perception, where other values apply, where experiences are classified differently than in everyday life. There is no being out of touch with reality and no separation from yourself and the world, on the contrary, the bond with yourself and the world becomes palpable.

Completeness

Subsequently, you experience yourself as a being that is perfectly okay. You experience yourself as part of the world, which is much greater than our finite minds can comprehend. What are mistakes? What are strengths? What is right? What is wrong? Who am I that I form an opinion about it?

It is how it is. This life is unique. This life is infinitely precious. This becomes as clear as day when you are no longer involved in the daily perspective which you are used to.

I know that so many people struggle with this existence, make no sense of it, become desperate. I can only encourage you to find a way to deal with all the pain and suffering. It is possible. Learn to appreciate little things.

Every person knows moments of doubt. Happiness and well-being don't always outweigh the painful experiences. Your path is not always clear to you. Whether happy or sorrowful, no matter which sides life shows you — inner peace is concealed beneath it.

No one has to ask the big question of being

Of course, not every Naikan participant asks questions of being, like: Where is my place in the world? Where am I in the big picture of it all? What is the meaning of my life? What comes after death? It is not necessary to come to Naikan with such existential questions. It's enough to want to get to know yourself better.

The question of life and death may come up

Sometimes, however, the subject of death comes to the fore. What happens then? As a Naikan guide you would be well advised to also be calm, stable and have an appreciative attitude on this topic.

It is quite common for me to be approached about the subject of death by Naikan participants. Perhaps they feel that I am not afraid of death. I have dealt with it and feel comfortable with the topic now. I have often experienced how relieving and liberating it was for my counterparts to finally have found someone to talk to about this profound topic.[25]

The big question of life and death is simply included in the Naikan method, whether one speaks about it or not. I see this as a great strength of Naikan.

8. Naikan — Can I know even more?

As with any method, there is an endless variety of observations, experiences and topics that are associated with the Naikan method. An entire world opens up.

There is a lot of information about the applications of Naikan and Naikan projects, most of it in German language. For a list of Naikan books — published in German or in English — see the chapter "Footnotes & Literature". You can find the current literature on Naikan on the Internet at http://naikan-literatur.info

Reading, talking, listening and being inspired by others is wonderful. But all this is useless if you do not think for yourself, see for yourself, and bring the information in connection with your own experiences. This is what I like about Naikan: The exercise is to discover your own truths.

What makes Naikan unlike other methods? What special effects does the Naikan method have? What principles is Naikan based on? Which questions and issues often emerge in connection with Naikan? What pitfalls does the method have? What can Naikan do particularly well?

These and similar questions move me, let me look again closely, and stimulate my mind. So let's dive into further thoughts on Naikan.

Where the 'I' and the 'you' come into contact

What are you actually focusing on in Naikan? My experience shows that Naikan is different from other methods, and I want to know why. So where does Naikan work?

The focus of the Naikan observation is what I have experienced with another person. The focus is always on the areas where I have come into contact with another person or with an environment: What have I experienced in contact with person X?

So I look at where the I and the you come into contact:

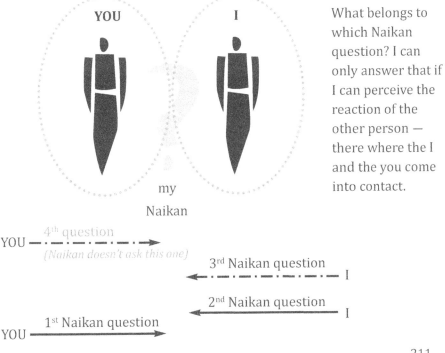

What belongs to which Naikan question? I can only answer that if I can perceive the reaction of the other person — there where the I and the you come into contact.

Come into contact

Naikan biography work, with the tool of the three questions, makes it possible to find connections with others without losing one's identity while doing so.

As humans we have two sides: On the one hand we are unique individuals and thus want to explore our own being and give it a form of expression. On the other hand, we are social creatures and depend on our environment, we cannot live without recognition and interaction. Naikan directs our attention to how we shape this social relationship.

Brain research says that 3 images are produced in the construction of reality in our brains:[26]

Image 1: Me inside (my body)
Image 2: The outside (the environment)
Image 3: The relationship between myself and the outside

The current sensations are processed in comparison with the stored memories in all three figures.

According to my observations, Naikan focuses on image 3: The relationship between myself and the outside and the comparison of the current sensations with the stored memories. (cf. previous image)

Recognizing the 'I' and the 'you'

Naikan is primarily focused on the points of contact between inside and outside. Realizations to increase knowledge about one's own inner world come up 'incidentally': motives, reasoning, desires, expectations, previous experiences, habits, behaviours, thoughts patterns, feelings... and so on. Gradually it shows what is happening IN ME — and I sometimes realize that my own inner life often acts up regardless of who is opposite me.

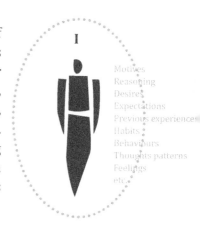

Perhaps the most pressing question regarding our counterpart is probably: Why did the other person do that? What was his motive? Sometimes you can actually see the motive of the other person. Most commonly, however, you have to recognize and accept the findings that you have obtained about the other person: That's just the way he is, that's his way of doing, his way of being. Although Naikan is clearly focused on the points of contact between the 'I' and the 'you', your own understanding of how YOU work inside can also grow 'incidentally'.

Check, recognize, change

Naikan includes levels of the mind and emotion, and a meta-level. The memories that are fed by mind and emotion are reviewed on a meta-level — the three Naikan questions sort out the memories, bring order to the perspectives, check what was (relevant) and what is. There is less understanding in the sense of, "I understand that," and more perception in the sense of, "I am this realization."

Alone the willingness to face your life experiences and to let them become conscious with the three Naikan questions, allows your experiences to be processed — even if the experience does not become conscious. Unconscious things are allowed to be part of life.

When memories come to mind, the images of the past may be compared to today's way of thinking. Reality and subjective pictures can be seen more clearly from a distance.

Sometimes the previous image is confirmed by today's perspective, but it is often recognized as a false image of reality. The aim is usually to get your own perspective closer to reality.

The images that we have of the past, of ourselves, and of others, are not set in stone. Naikan trains you to see reality and your own picture of reality, and to change it if need be.[27] Internal and external changes are a natural part of life.

*Truth!
Everybody believes they know the truth; and everybody knows a different truth.*

Gotthold Ephraim Lessing

From either this or that…
to both this and that

We humans are usually fixed on thinking in categories, "either this or that". For example, I either cause this person difficulties now (3rd Naikan question) OR I do something for this person (2nd Naikan question). We tend to believe that there is only one valid response.

It is very difficult for us to think: I am now causing this person difficulties in this respect and I am doing something for them AT THE SAME TIME. And this person is doing something for me also AT THE SAME TIME. This means that we slowly have to learn that several things are present or happen simultaneously, not "either this or that," but "both this and that".

In the Naikan week it is usually a lengthy process until you realize that several Naikan questions can be answered at the same time when you are focusing on a particular situation or person. Keep in mind that you are in a laboratory situation in a sense in a Naikan retreat, in a protected atmosphere where you can concentrate on the finer points of perception. If the "both this and that" is already difficult in a retreat, how much harder will it be in everyday life?

When we leave the silence and return to daily life, so many impressions are thrown upon us, we have to handle so many things at once. Are we also aware in everyday stress that many things run simultaneously? It is so easy to fall back into the usual thinking of "either this or that ".

It is therefore important to continue training. Practising Naikan means training our own perception so that we can notice more and more how many different things are actually present simultaneously.

The eternal question of blame

What's to blame? Wikipedia says: Blame is the act of censuring, holding responsible, making negative statements about an individual or group that their action or actions are socially or morally irresponsible, the opposite of praise.[28] Naikan thinks: It is necessary to identify whether you yourself were the cause of unpleasantness. This is why you ask the 3rd Naikan question: What difficulties have I caused? It is important to take responsibility for your part. Either I am responsible — to blame — for something, or not. It's about having this clarity.

This is something quite different from our usual vague guilt. If I have feelings of guilt, it means that I still hope that it might be different. Had I just not done that, had I just done it differently, none of this would have happened… There is an ideal image in your mind, which reality does not correspond to. That means that I still haven't said "yes" to what I have experienced.

Naikan means accepting what was and what is, whether it was pleasant or unpleasant. Naikan shows that you're a human with flaws, weaknesses and shortcomings. But this by no means causes blame or guilt. On the contrary, by recognizing your own shortcomings you can take responsibility for what you've done — and only for what you've done, nothing more and nothing less.

Our own inability to recognize and take responsibility for our actions means that we can work on it from now on.

If you can accept yourself as a human being with flaws, weaknesses and shortcomings, then you become more lenient with the weaknesses of others. Of course you can see when people make mistakes, you should also react accordingly, but there is no need for drama to come of it. Because the other person is also only human, and humans make mistakes.

What is tolerance?
It is a necessary consequence of humanity.
We are all fallible, let us then
pardon each other's follies.

Voltaire

The step towards reconciliation

When people talk about their Naikan experiences, they often speak about the reconciling power of Naikan in a very touching manner.[29]

What's reconciliation? To forgive and forget is certainly not meant by it. On the contrary, it is about seeing how one's life was, how others have acted, and how you yourself have acted. It is about accepting what you have experienced. That is essential.

We cannot change our fellow human beings and reality. What we can change is our way of looking at what has happened and what is happening now. It is futile to wish that the past would have been different. We can neither undo our own mistakes, nor painful experiences, or inadequacies of our mother, father, partner or whomever. Naikan helps you to accept what you have experienced as part of the past.

Reconciliation does not mean ignoring painful experiences or mistakes that have happened to you or someone else. You have to give the feeling — that something was wrong — some space to breathe. The phases of pain, of accusations, and of anger are part of it. The irreconcilable cannot just be skipped, it is an intermediate step towards reconciliation. It is also not about excuses or apologies.

Naikan helps you to look at yourself and others the way they are — with all the rough edges. Life is simply not perfect. Living based on this understanding allows you to face yourself and the world with more tolerance.

The step towards reconciliation in Naikan is not a mental decision, but an inner feeling of acceptance.

You cannot force it, it happens at its own pace. A prerequisite is the willingness to see and accept what was and what is. If you succeed, you will feel relieved and at peace with yourself and the world.

The thing called gratitude

Naikan is associated with gratitude remarkably often.[30] Through the practise of Naikan many people become aware of how much they have received in their lives and how little they had noticed it before. The focus is drawn to the fullness of life and what you have experienced. The desire to say thank you often arises from the inside. It is usually a simple thank you in recognition of what one has learned. Sometimes it is a deeply felt sense of gratitude that is experienced as a source of happiness and satisfaction.

Unfortunately, Naikan is often misunderstood by the clear link to gratitude. I repeatedly meet people who think: I will do Naikan and will become grateful. Or even more grave: I must become grateful through Naikan.

I remember a Naikan participant who had just worked through some quite difficult memories in Naikan, and literally said to me in a desperate manner: "And I have to be grateful for this?!"

No, no one should or must be grateful for anything. You can neither prescribe that, nor enforce it. Gratitude simply arises. Or not. Both are fine.

It is true that Naikan fosters the emergence of gratitude.[31] You do intensely concern yourself with what you have been given from others with the 1st Naikan question. Sooner or later you will realize: It was all there for me. One can neither determine nor foresee when this warm feeling, called gratitude, will arise.

Perhaps you may never feel gratitude for some of the things that you have experienced in your life. That is also okay. It is perfectly adequate if you can accept that things were as they were. It is the way it is. That's all.

The past and the here and now

What is the point of looking at the past if we live in the here and now? I am often asked this question. The Naikan answer is that we can only completely live in the present if we recognize the past, accept it, and free ourselves from it.

At this moment, in the here and now, our whole past is present — we forget that far too often. What makes me the way I am today is what I have already experienced.[32]

We all know the situation when we are in the here and now, but we respond in a way that has nothing to do with the here and now. Instead, there is quite simply an automatism running, which we have become accustomed to in the past.

Naikan allows us to recognize these automatisms first in retrospect, that they are then transparent in the here and now. We recognize ourselves by looking at the past, so that we are controlled less and less by the automatic filters from the past. This means freedom, because new perspectives arise by recognizing the filter and we then have the choice to do things differently — now.

Getting to grips with what happened in the past allows us to make the present more livable. Staying in the past and rethinking everything over and over is counterproductive. Naikan helps to look at the past one more time, and then learn from it. And with practise, you will be able to focus on what you have received, what you have given, and what difficulties you have caused, in the here and now.

Every trifle is an experience for an imaginative person.

Julius Leopold Klein

Nothing special

Naikan is something special, something great, something extraordinary. How many people venture into the adventure of getting to know themselves, with all the good and bad sides? And how many people have such a simple and clear method like Naikan available to do it? If you look at it in this way, then Naikan is something special, a gift.

The deep Naikan practise paradoxically begins when one is not expecting anything special. Because Naikan is nothing special, nothing great, nothing extraordinary. If you examine something, draw your attention to your own inner world, listen to your own inner voice, then this can be just as commonplace as washing yourself and brushing your teeth. As unspectacular as brushing your teeth is, that's how inconspicuous introspection can be. An example: 1. What has X done for me? She asked me a question. 2. What have I done for X ? I answered it. 3. What difficulties have I caused? She looked a little bored, maybe I was too detailed in my answer. Maybe you're thinking that if it is so mundane, then why do Naikan?

Yes, why? To stay with the previous example, if you think of how many conflicts arise because one doesn't give or receive an answer. Think of how many discords arise because a question was not asked. Mundane little things often have large effects. That is why it is always worthwhile to look at the little things in everyday life with Naikan.

Learn to enjoy looking at everyday things, like you might look at a work of art or a natural spectacle. You will be wealthy and rewarded by doing so.

Freedom

"Practising Naikan all senses become clear, and we are freed from entanglements."[33] The Japanese Naikan guide Prof. Akira Ishii sees one of the essential effects of Naikan as allowing you to see a different view of reality. Usually we see everything through our own lenses, through our expectations, beliefs, desires, etc. But how did our behaviour actually come across to the other person?

There is a big difference between the image that others have of us and our own self-image. In Naikan you learn how you are seen by the other person, you learn to see yourself from the other side. You turn your observation inward. This makes it possible to accept one's own past. Since the present is a result of the past, accepting the past means also accepting the present.

You no longer feel trapped by your own history, but you free yourself of it.

Freedom also arises in that ideals come under scrutiny through Naikan. One usually has an ideal image of oneself, of others, of certain situations and so on — so it must be true! You examine the facts in Naikan, the actual image, the reality, and you learn to accept this. If you have a more realistic view of yourself and the world, your own space to manoeuvre grows, it creates freedom in thought and action.

You are on your own in Naikan. No one else tells you what to do, you find the answers yourself. It is not necessarily pleasant to not have anyone tell you what you should and shouldn't do. This form of self-determination and freedom needs some getting used to.

A Naikan participant brought this to the point when I asked him how he was doing. He said, "Strange, because I can just be how I am."

> *A great lesson that one can often learn,
> is the confession of one's own inadequacy.*
>
> Denis Diderot

Misunderstood Naikan

Just as with every other method, there are also misunderstandings that frequently arise regarding Naikan.

Misunderstanding no. 1: The 4th question is not allowed.

Naikan participants often think that they have to leave out the fourth question — Who has caused me difficulties? — because Naikan only works with three questions. This is nonsense. Of course it is important to recognize where problems, damage or pain was contributed by external sources. Naikan simply teaches you not to focus your thoughts and feelings on the problems, but to always pay attention to the possibilities. Perceiving, recognizing, and then consciously controlling what you focus your attention on.

Misunderstanding no. 2: I will not cause any more difficulties.

Yes, I too had this aspiration at the beginning — and I failed miserably. Because the fact is that you, as a human being, cause difficulties. I can and will do my best to cause less problems, but they may and will still arise.

I was once asked in an interview what consequence the third question has. Should it make me refrain from causing others difficulties?

No. The third question is for you to recognize and acknowledge that you are a person who also causes difficulties, you are not perfect. This is actually a big relief. But it is primarily about seeing that what you have done causes somebody else problems.

Just because it was well-intentioned, doesn't meant that is was good for the other person. If I am aware that the other person has difficulties with my words or my behaviour, then I can also deal with it differently. Naikan trains the perception and compassion for yourself and others.

Living Naikan

Naikan opens many insights. These insights allow your appreciation for your unique ability to grow, for the good of the community, and the world.[34] Knowing is one thing. Acting on these insights is another.

Living Naikan means not seeking your own path from external sources, but reflecting on your own inner resources and values. And always keeping in mind that your own actions have an effect on other people and the world.

Do you want to remain passive and accept life? Or do you want to use your energy trying to create your own life in many ways? It's your choice, each time anew.

If everyday life stresses you out, bores you, annoys you, or under or overwhelms you, don't complain, do Naikan and get yourself out of there. Ask yourself the 1st Naikan question: What have I received? Who does something for me?

If something bothers, annoys, or angers you, or even makes you feel helpless, don't complain, do Naikan and get yourself out of there. Ask yourself the 2nd Naikan question: What can I do? And ask yourself the 3rd Naikan question: What difficulties have I caused?

Train yourself to have a clear view of the inner and outer world with Naikan. This clarity will allow to do what is appropriate in each situation.

> The sun so hot,
> the pressure so strong,
> the heart so small,
> the heart so tender,
> the heart breaks,
> it seems refreshed by the light,
> refreshed, nourished, conductive.
> Life in transition,
> good and evil,
> right, wrong.
> Who cares?
> Who? Who?
> Good luck, wanderer.
>
> *Untitled. By Jan J.*

9. Naikan — Where can I attend a retreat?

There are several Naikan centres in Austria and Germany where you can attend a Naikan week, as well as other Naikan providers and deals. In addition, there are several Naikan weeks in Switzerland and other European countries. There are Naikan places in the United States and several Naikan centres in Japan. A list of current Naikan contact addresses all over the world can be found on the Internet, for example on http://naikan.ws/english/naikan-links.html

Have a look at the websites or the information material of different Naikan providers. If you feel drawn to an offer, then this is usually the best choice. Trust your inner feeling here. If you are unsure or need more information please contact a Naikan guide for a personal consultation.

Consider whether you would like to practise Naikan in a group room or in a single room, or whether both variants are suitable for you.

There are Naikan venues in rural areas where you can take short walks, and in the city where it is not recommended to go outside. If you need movement or trees around you then choose an appropriate venue.

Naikan is suitable for people of all ages. The only requirement for Naikan is to be able to distinguish between memory and reality, and fantasy and fiction. Thus, Naikan is not suitable for people with cognitive disorders, psychosis, or dementia. If you are currently in medical or psychotherapeutic treatment you should consult your therapist about participating in Naikan.

If you want to experience the power of silence and learn an easy way for your own inner research, then nothing stands in the way of your Naikan week.

How can I prepare for my Naikan retreat?

Before your Naikan retreat you should do everything to the point that you do not have to worry about the outside world during this time. You should inform your family and your workplace that you will be unavailable for a while. Give a close friend of yours the contact details of the Naikan centre if you want to be reached in the case of an emergency. Set your voice mail and e-mail to let people know that you are temporarily away.

There is nothing special to consider with regard to how you should spend the time before the Naikan week. If you arrive very tired then just take your time and relax at the retreat. You decide the pace and intensity of the exercises in the Naikan week. The daily routine gives you a structure that allows you to find your individual tempo.

Basically, you do not need content preparation before a Naikan retreat. If you do wish to prepare a little, then you can busy yourself with your life story. One possibility is to take notes about your own life so that the work with your memory can run even more relaxed. How old were you in which year, where did you live? Which events can you recall (e.g. changing schools, moving…)?

You can create a list of those individuals who have played a role in your life. You can look at old photos as a reminder…

The best preparation is to throw all possible expectations out the window. Just be curious about yourself. Everything else can be found during the Naikan exercise.

One no longer has enough soliloquies nowadays. One is probably afraid of telling oneself one's own opinion.

Jean Giraudoux

What I can expect at a Naikan retreat

I arrive at a Naikan centre. I am greeted warmly and am invited to eat something. I can meet the other Naikan participants before we begin. It is good that you can briefly get to know the other participants because you will not have any contact during the Naikan retreat.

The Naikan guide will give us an introduction after the meal: How does it work? What do I actually have to do when practising Naikan?

I find out that I'm going to be spending most of the time at my exercise space. I can sit, lay, or stand there, there is no prescribed way to practise. Sitting is recommended because it is better for concentration. I am asked to behave quietly when other Naikan participants are in the same room as me. Everyone should be able to practise Naikan undisturbed. In order for me to be completely involved in my introspection and not bother other participants, I agree to the following things during Naikan: no reading, no listening to the radio, no television, no phone, no computer, no contact with people outside the Naikan centre, silence among participants.

There are no regulations other than those; merely recommendations.

There is, for example, the recommendation to spend as much time at your exercise space as possible, because this allows protection and improved concentration. However, I can leave my exercise space at any time, whether it be to go get a little fresh air, fetch some tea, or to go smoke a cigarette.

Eating and drinking: Beverages and fruit are always at the ready, which I can take at any time during the Naikan retreat. Breakfast, lunch and dinner are brought to you by the Naikan guide on a tray. You are taken care of all around.

Let us begin the Naikan introspection.

I retreat to my small practise space, which will provide me with refuge and protection during my stay. No one will bother me here, only the Naikan guide comes to me for my individual Naikan conversation.

I begin with Naikan just as it was explained to me in the introduction.

Naikan begins with the focus on my mother or on the person who took on the mother role. So I try to remember the first years of my life (when I was 0-6 years old, in other words from my first memory to the start of school), search for memories associated with my mother, and match those memories with the 3 Naikan questions.

1. What did my mother do for me in this time period?
2. What did I do for my mother in this time period?
3. What difficulties did I cause my mother in this time period?

After 60 to 90 minutes, in which I shovelled through my memories, the Naikan guide comes to me for my individual Naikan conversation. I tell her some concrete situations that I recall about my mother in my preschool years for each of the three Naikan questions. We speak at a normal level in the single room. We would whisper in a group room so that the other Naikan participants are not disturbed. The Naikan guide thanks me, we agree on how to continue with Naikan, and I'm already back to working on my memories and myself. The Naikan conversation lasts about 5 to 10 minutes.

Thereafter I focus on my mother in elementary school, when I was 6-10 years old. I consider concrete events which I can remember. I again have at least one hour time for this. Naikan conversation, Naikan practise, Naikan conversation... Time period for time period, I structure the memories from the beginning to the present moment, or until the person who I am focusing on left my life.

This is how it goes on and on. After my mother comes my father, then my siblings, grandparents, partners, friends, colleagues, specific topics... Which people and issues I focus on, depends on my life story and my current life situation.

I will sometimes concentrate more, and sometimes less during my Naikan week. In the introduction the Naikan guide mentioned that one can also go through tedious phases and experience real blocks. She said that some don't have this at all, and some think about whether Naikan has any meaning every day, and if they should not rather go home. I'm probably in the middle because I only occasionally think about leaving, a real crisis does not occur.

Sometimes I need movement, a few quiet physical exercises at my space loosen me up. Maybe I'll get some fresh air, let's see. I look forward to the food each time it comes, it is vegetarian and delicious. It also brings a little variation to the Naikan day, which is otherwise devoted to reflection and inner work. You would not believe how hungry thinking makes you.

Although the Naikan talks are short, I'm glad that someone is here for me. In the beginning I think very carefully about what I am going to say in the conversations, but in the course of the week I become more and more relaxed. I sometimes decide to tell the guide something which may be very difficult for me to admit. Just because no one judges me for it. That's kind of liberating.

Later in the week the thoughts already revolve around how I can apply what I have learned in everyday life. I alternate between uncertainty and confidence that I can change something for myself.

I slowly emerge from the peace and silence at the end of the Naikan retreat. There is a final talk with all the Naikan participants. We can talk about our experiences during the week and the Naikan guide gives us plenty of advice and tips for everyday life back home.

Closing the door on change means closing the door on life...
Walt Whitman

What should I be aware of after the Naikan retreat?

Prepare yourself for the fact that you will need time to adjust to the fast and demanding everyday life after the retreat and the silence. It is recommended to have at least one full day off following the Naikan week. Give yourself time to adjust.

After that it can be helpful to fulfil your full capabilities again, so that you get back into your daily routine well.

Some Naikan participants get back into their everyday life rapidly and almost unnoticed. Some people experience the transition more intensely, feelings or thoughts remain in your body and mind for a few more days, sometimes you have unexpected mood swings. That is quite normal after a long period of introspection. Don't worry, the feelings and thoughts calm down by themselves.

I am often asked the following at the end of the Naikan retreat: Will what I have realized and recognized stay with me, or will it disappear again? The findings definitely stay, even if they are not constantly conscious. You have made some order internally.

You have changed your view of the world — the world, however, remains the same. Maybe some people react differently to you than you are used to.

Perhaps you decided that everything will be different from now on. Don't expect too much change in your everyday life. Do not be disappointed if old habits come back — recognizing this is already very valuable.

Some things change by themselves after Naikan, and some things that you really want to change take a lot of work. After the intense week of Naikan the practise in everyday life follows, where your insights begin to act and where you can begin to act accordingly. Therefore, at the end of the Naikan week we say the following: Naikan starts now!

Epilogue

After the countless words that I have written in this book, I want to encourage you once again to experience Naikan for yourself. Because one's own experience is much better than any theory — always. No one can take what you have experienced away from you. It is up to you how you deal with your experiences.

You now know about Naikan. It is in your hands to decide what you will do with it.

How can we make Naikan more well-known?

We often busy ourselves with this question in our Naikan groups. Providing high-quality information and trusting that many people will inspire others with their Naikan experiences — that still seems the most appropriate in order to draw attention to Naikan. That is also why you are holding this book in your hand.

A few years ago, Gitti F. wrote an advertising text about Naikan, which I always find worth reading. I am pleased that she has allowed me to use it.

Naikan Specials!

by Gitti F.

If you were to put this task in the hands of marketing strategists of major communication companies, concepts along the lines of "Increase of scope by target group programming" would probably emerge:

SAFARI NAIKAN: Book your Naikan adventure! Seven days of Naikan in Kenya! Every participant sits in his own hut in the kraal. You'll be surprised who will come to the conversation — a Naikan guide? A rhinoceros? A lion? We recommend taking out risk insurance.

ISLAND NAIKAN: Divine Naikan on the Seychelles! You will sit on your own little island for seven days. Guaranteed biological produce, the machete to open coconuts is included. Shower time is replaced by the monsoon rains.

VIDEO NAIKAN: There is a monitor behind the Naikan screen. The Naikan guide appears when it is time for your conversation. You can develop your own script using the three Naikan questions.

NAIKAN VIDEO: The ideal addition to a Naikan week. Do your Naikan at home while watching TV. The video shows a Naikan venue from inside. The screen suddenly opens and our revered Master Ishii-Sensei bows and asks the famous question, "What are you focusing on?". You get the video in three fitting lengths: 60, 70 or 90 minutes. Also available in an elegant leather pouch as a special edition.

NAIKAN DIET: Ask the three Naikan questions with the focus being on any dish. For example: "What has the chocolate done for me? What have I done for the chocolate? What difficulties have I caused the chocolate?" You will definitely have lost your appetite after 60 minutes.

An accompanying advertising campaign would aggressively have to advertise in the newspapers:

OUR OFFER — YOUR CHANCE! Highest rewards for only seven days of work! Bring your application and a little of your own money and we will create the framework for your successful future. Board and lodging will be supplied. Have the courage to take risks and get more information at your local Naikan centre (phone, address, opening times, etc.).

STOP! Thankfully, I realize that we have all been spared these adds. The end doesn't justify the means, and so the traditional recipe to spread Naikan will remain: Practise a week and live this experience as an example.

Gitti F. has been practising Naikan since 1993 and has extensive experience in the media industry.

Naikan cannot promise anything

Naikan has no ideology, there is no predetermined destination, and no answers from the outside. And no one knows in advance, which answers will show up from the inside. That is why Naikan cannot promise anything. And that, in turn, is hardly conducive to an advertising strategy.

At the same time, it is a great strength of Naikan to be a method without ideologies and without a predetermined destination. Because of this, those people who are not looking for answers on the outside, but are willing to explore their own depths, feel addressed to take part, at their own pace, according to their very own character.

Thank you

At this point I would like to express my gratitude to the people in my family and in my friendship circle — thank you for believing in me, supporting me in difficult moments, motivating me, laughing with me and sharing my joy.

Many thanks to my Naikan teachers, my Naikan participants and my Naikan friends who have given me wonderful moments and touching insights into human beings, who trusted me, and who allowed me to more deeply understand Naikan in many ways.

Dear reader: Thank you for reading my words with an open mind. I wish you all the best in cultivating your inner dialogue and mastering your daily routine with peace of mind. If Naikan happens to be helpful in doing so, then I am more than happy about it.

*The time
of the other's interpretation will come,
and
no word will be left upon them.*

Rainer Maria Rilke

Footnotes & Literature

Footnotes

[1] Luise Reddemann describes many of our inner signals and characteristics and shows how one can find peaceful ways of dealing with them through pausing and taking a break. Reddemann, Luise: *Eine Reise von 1.000 Meilen beginnt mit dem ersten Schritt. Seelische Kräfte entwickeln und fördern.* Freiburg im Breisgau 2010. Book only available in German.

[2] Detlev Bölter deals with Naikan in terms of epistemological basics of how memory is stored, how reality is created in us. He draws on the constructivist worldview to do so. Bölter, Detlev: *Drei Fragen, die die Welt verändern.* Bielefeld 2004. Book only available in German.

[3] Fumon S. Nakagawa illuminates the term "repentance" (Sange), which is understood quite differently in the West than it is in the Japanese culture. In Japan, repentance is tantamount to recognition and goes hand in hand with a change of behaviour. Nakagawa, Fumon S.: *Zen – Weil wir Menschen sind.* Berlin 2003. Book only available in German.

[4] The quotations by Ishin Yoshimoto were taken from Hartl, Josef; Schuh, Johanna: *Die Naikan Methode.* Wien 1998. Book only available in German.

[5] An illuminating and inspiring insight into the diversity of our excuses is given by: Roser, Brigitte: *Das Ende der Ausreden.* München 2010. Book only available in German.

[6] Thich Nhat Hanh: *The Heart of the Buddha's teachings.* (Rider: 1999, page 24). Thich Nhat Hanh describes the basics of Buddhism in simple and clear wording.

[7] Anthroposophy has a beneficial way of looking at human development, and it recognizes, in contrast to many other theories of development, developmental phases through the entire adult life. Burkhard, Gudrun: *Taking Charge: Your Life Patterns and Their Meaning.*

[8] Those who are interested in a practical presentation of ethics in everyday life, including lying and stealing, will enjoy this book on ethical rules of Buddhism: Rizzetto, Diane Eshin: *Waking Up to What You Do.*

[9] Reiunken Shue Usami is a Japanese Zen master who sees Naikan as a deep practise of Sanghe (repentance) and has developed the Jujukinkai retreat from a combination Naikan, Zen and Jujukinkai (Buddhist ethics). The fundamentals of the practise in his temple can be found in: Reiunken Shue Usami, Osho Noriyuki Usami: *Living Vibrantly with Peace of Mind.* Norderstedt 2013

[10] Bauer, Joachim: *Prinzip Menschlichkeit. Warum wir von Natur aus kooperieren.* Hamburg 2007, page 37. Book only available in German.

[11] Picard, Max: *Die Welt des Schweigens.* Frankfurt am Main 1959, page 15. In English: Max Picard (Author), Stanley Godwin (Translator): *The World of Silence.*

[12] Nagashima, Masahiro, in: Müller-Ebeling, Claudia; Steinke, Gerald (Ed.): *Naikan Praxisbuch I.* Bielefeld 2004, page 151. Book only available in German.

[13] Numerous practical Naikan tips can be found in: Schuh, Johanna (Ed.): *Naikan im Alltag – Ruhe und Kraft für jeden Tag.* Norderstedt 2012. Book only available in German.

[14] If you want to deepen your knowledge on this subject, Sabine Kaspari devotes an entire chapter to Naikan with regard to marriage and partnership. The term "confrontation with the present" explains Naikan with regard to children, as well as Naikan with the focus on your professional life. Kaspari, Sabine: *Naikan – Die Kraft der Versöhnung: Mit der buddhistischen 3-Fragen-Methode zu innerem Frieden.* München 2012. Book only available in German.

[15] A lot of literature has been published about practising mindfulness and awareness, which comes from Buddhism. "We do not get better, we only become more free," through mindful practise, said: Kolk, Sylvia in her book: *Segeln im Sturm. Mit Leidenschaft den spirituellen Alltag meistern.* Bielefeld 2009. Book only available in German.

[16] If you appreciate a variety of ideas on how you can regain strength in everyday life, then you will find plenty of ideas in: Münchhausen, Marco from the book: *Wo die Seele auftankt. Die besten Möglichkeiten, Ihre Ressourcen zu aktivieren.* München 2006. Book only available in German.

[17] Brenda Shoshanna sees Naikan as a technique that enriches Zen practise. Brenda Shoshanna: *Zen Miracles: Finding Peace in an Insane World.*

[18] You can find a wide range of application areas and effects of Naikan in: Müller-Ebeling, Claudia; Steinke, Gerald (Ed.): *Naikan: Versöhnung mit sich selbst.* Bielefeld 2003. Book only available in German.

[19] cf. Bölter, Detlev: *Drei Fragen, die die Welt verändern.* Bielefeld 2004, page 39. Book only available in German.

[20] Chikako Ozawa-De Silva has dealt specifically with Naikan with regard to the anthropological aspect and worked out which elements of Naikan apply to Japanese culture and which don't. Ozawa-De Silva, Chikako: *Psychotherapy and Religion in Japan: The Japanese Introspection Practice of Naikan.* New York 2006

[21] The emergence of Naikan is described in detail in: Hartl, Josef; Schuh, Johanna: *Die Naikan Methode.* Wien 1998. Book only available in German. In addition, there is a free e-book on http://www.naikan-literatur.info/gratis-e-books

[22] cf. http://www.ramakrishna.de/japan/naikan.php (on 02.02.2014) This website describes the history of Naikan and basic information about Jōdo Shinshū (Reines-Land-Buddhismus). Website only available in German.

[23] cf. Ozawa-De Silva, Chikako: *Psychotherapy and Religion in Japan: The Japanese Introspection Practice of Naikan.* New York 2006, page 26. An excellent book that elaborates on cultural (Japanese), spiritual (Buddhist) and methodological aspects of Naikan.

[24] Ishii, Prof. Akira. *Recommendations for Naikan.* Free eBook on http://www.naikan-literatur.info/gratis-e-books

[25] If you want to come to terms with dying, death and dealing with it then read: Longaker, Christine: *Facing Death and Finding Hope: A Guide to the Emotional and Spiritual Care of the Dying.*

[26] cf. Bauer, Joachim: *Das Gedächtnis des Körpers.* Frankfurt/Main 2002. Book only available in German.

[27] cf. Ozawa-De Silva, Chikako: *Psychotherapy and Religion in Japan: The Japanese Introspection Practice of Naikan.* New York 2006, page 79.
[28] https://en.wikipedia.org/wiki/Blame (on 01.11.2015)
[29] Two Naikan books about reconciliation have been published by two different authors: Kaspari, Sabine: *Naikan – Die Kraft der Versöhnung: Mit der buddhistischen 3-Fragen-Methode zu innerem Frieden.* München 2012. And: Müller-Ebeling, Claudia; Steinke, Gerald (Ed.): *Naikan: Versöhnung mit sich selbst.* Bielefeld 2003. Both books only available in German.
[30] Gregg Krech wrote a practical book in the USA, with the focus on Naikan and gratitude, which shows many ways that Naikan can be practised in everyday life. It suggests that Naikan creates warmth and clarity. Gregg Krech: *Naikan: Gratitude, Grace, and the Japanese Art of Self-Reflection.* Berkeley 2002. In the German language: Krech, Gregg: *Die Kraft der Dankbarkeit. Die spirituelle Praxis des Naikan im Alltag.* Berlin 2003
[31] cf. Robert Emmons: *Thanks!: How the New Science of Gratitude Can Make You Happier.* Naikan is listed as one of the ways through which you can promote gratitude. Boston/New York 2007. Barbara Stöckl devotes a chapter of her book to the Naikan method: Stöckl, Barbara: *Wofür soll ich dankbar sein?* Salzburg 2012. Book only available in German.
[32] cf. Emmons, Robert: *Vom Glück, dankbar zu sein.* Frankfurt/Main 2008, page 187. In English: Robert Emmons: *Thanks!: How the New Science of Gratitude Can Make You Happier.*
[33] Ishii, Prof. Akira. *Recommendations for Naikan.* Free eBook on http://www.naikan-literatur.info/gratis-e-books
[34] cf. Nishida, Norimasa: *Naikan Self-Reflection for Happiness and Success.* Japan 2001. Norimasa Nishida describes the many effects of Naikan on everyday life in family and professional life.

Literature

Bauer, Joachim: *Das Gedächtnis des Körpers.* Eichborn, Frankfurt/Main 2002

Bauer, Joachim: *Prinzip Menschlichkeit. Warum wir von Natur aus kooperieren.* Hoffmann und Campe, Hamburg 2007

Burkhard, Gudrun: *Das Leben in die Hand nehmen, Arbeit an der eigenen Biographie.* Freies Geistesleben, Stuttgart 2000. In English: *Taking Charge: Your Life Patterns and Their Meaning.* Floris Books, Edinburgh 1997.

Emmons, Robert: *Vom Glück, dankbar zu sein.* Campus, Frankfurt/Main 2008. Originally in English: Robert Emmons: *Thanks!: How the New Science of Gratitude Can Make You Happier.* Houghton Mifflin Harcourt, Boston/New York 2007

Hartl-Margreiter, Helga (Ed.), Reiunken Shue Usami, Osho Noriyuki Usami: *Lebendig leben mit Frieden im Geist. Über Tradition und Praxis des Shin-Buddhistischen Tempels Senkobo.* Books on Demand, Norderstedt 2013. Originally in English: Reiunken Shue Usami, Osho Noriyuki Usami: *Living Vibrantly with Peace of Mind.*

Kolk, Sylvia: *Segeln im Sturm. Mit Leidenschaft den spirituellen Alltag meistern.* Theseus, Bielefeld 2009

Kornfield, Jack: *Das weise Herz. Die universellen Prinzipien buddhistischer Psychologie.* Arkana, München 2008. Originally in English: Jack Kornfield: *The Wise Heart: A Guide to the Universal Teachings of Buddhist Psychology.*

Longaker, Christine: *Dem Tod begegnen und Hoffnung finden. Die emotionale und spirituelle Begleitung Sterbender.* Piper, München 2001. Originally in English: Christine Longaker: *Facing Death and Finding Hope: A Guide to the Emotional and Spiritual Care of the Dying.*

Münchhausen, Marco von: *Wo die Seele auftankt. Die besten Möglichkeiten, Ihre Ressourcen zu aktivieren.* Goldmann, München 2006

Nakagawa, Fumon S.: *Zen – Weil wir Menschen sind.* Theseus, Berlin 2003

Picard, Max: *Die Welt des Schweigens.* Fischer, Frankfurt am Main 1959. In English: Max Picard (Author), Stanley Godwin (Translator): *The World of Silence.*

Reddemann, Luise: *Eine Reise von 1.000 Meilen beginnt mit dem ersten Schritt. Seelische Kräfte entwickeln und fördern.* Herder, Freiburg im Breisgau 2010

Rizzetto, Diane Eshin: *Zen für jeden Tag.* Knaur, München 2009. Originally in English: Diane Eshin Rizzetto: *Waking Up to What You Do: A Zen Practice for Meeting Every Situation with Intelligence and Compassion.*

Roser, Brigitte: *Das Ende der Ausreden.* Diana, München 2010

Shoshanna, Brenda: *Zen-Wunder.* Goldmann, München 2003. Originally in English: Brenda Shoshanna: *Zen Miracles: Finding Peace in an Insane World.*

Stöckl, Barbara: *Wofür soll ich dankbar sein?* Ecowin, Salzburg 2012

Thich Nhat Hanh: *Das Herz von Buddhas Lehre.* Herder, Freiburg im Breisgau 2010. Originally in English: Thich Nhat Hanh: *The Heart of the Buddha's Teaching: Transforming Suffering into Peace, Joy, and Liberation.*

Literature on Naikan

Bölter, Detlev: *Drei Fragen, die die Welt verändern.* Kamphausen, Bielefeld 2004

Dittschar, Wilhelm; Ishii, Akira: *Naikan in der Schule.* Kamphausen, Bielefeld 2008

Hartl, Josef; Schuh, Johanna: *Die Naikan Methode.* Naikido, Wien 1998

Kaspari, Sabine: *Naikan – Die Kraft der Versöhnung: Mit der buddhistischen 3-Fragen-Methode zu innerem Frieden.* Gräfe und Unzer, München 2012

Kaspari, Sabine; Lendawitsch, Margit; Ritter Franz (Ed.): *NAIKAN Eintauchen ins Sein. 50 Jahre Methode Naikan. Neue Wege zu sich selbst finden.* Books on Demand, Norderstedt 2015

Krech, Gregg: *Naikan: Gratitude, Grace, and the Japanese Art of Self-Reflection.* Stone Bridge Press, Berkeley 2002

Krech, Gregg: *Die Kraft der Dankbarkeit. Die spirituelle Praxis des Naikan im Alltag.* Theseus, Berlin 2003

Müller-Ebeling, Claudia; Steinke, Gerald (Ed.): *Naikan: Versöhnung mit sich selbst.* Kamphausen, Bielefeld 2003

Müller-Ebeling, Claudia; Steinke, Gerald (Ed.): *Naikan Praxisbuch I.* Kamphausen, Bielefeld 2004

Niehaus, Gerburgis A.: *Konflikte lösen mit 3 Fragen. Neue Impulse durch die "Cappuccinoblick-Methode" für wirkungsvolle Prozesse in Coaching, Beratung & Teamarbeit.* Ökotopia, Münster 2015

Nishida, Norimasa: *Naikan Self-Reflection for Happiness and Success.* Toyoko Inn, Japan 2001 (Book is only available in Toyoko Inn Hotels)

Ozawa-De Silva, Chikako: *Psychotherapy and Religion in Japan: The Japanese Introspection Practice of Naikan.* Routledge, New York 2006

Reiss, Wolfram; Bechmann, Ulrike (Ed.): *Selbstbetrachtung hinter Gittern. Naikan im Strafvollzug in Deutschland und Österreich.* Tectum, Marburg 2016

Schuh, Johanna (Ed.): *Naikan im Alltag – Ruhe und Kraft für jeden Tag.* Books on Demand, Norderstedt 2012

Current Naikan books, literature und E-books: http://naikan-literatur.info

Living Naikan means living everyday life very carefully.

Ishin Yoshimoto

„Naikan" – calligraphy by Ishin Yoshimoto, the founder of Naikan

*Born as a human being,
I am learning to be human my whole life.*

Johanna Schuh

About the Author

Johanna Schuh, born in 1968, has been working as a Naikan guide since 2000. She founded the Insightvoice Naikan Center in Vienna in 2005, which she has since been directing.

QUESTION: How did you come about Naikan and how long have you been busying yourself with it?

SCHUH: I met Naikan guide Josef Hartl (1961-2005) in 1991, and heard about the Naikan method from him. In January 1993, I first practised a Naikan week with him, in August 1993 a second week followed under the direction of Professor Akira Ishii. In 1994 I started to assist in Naikan and to intensively busy myself with the method by practising myself and accompanying Naikan participants as an assistant. In 1996 I wrote my thesis at the Academy for Social Work in Vienna — "Naikan as a methodical way in social work?". I published a book called "The Naikan Method" with Josef Hartl in 1998.

QUESTION: How long have you been working as a Naikan guide?

SCHUH: I started the training as a Naikan guide in 1994, under Josef and Helga Hartl at "The Naikanhouse" in Vienna and Lower Austria, and Prof. Akira Ishii who is from Japan. I have been working as an independent Naikan guide since 2000 and have been running the Insightvoice Naikan Centre in Vienna since 2005.

QUESTION: What effect does Naikan have in your opinion?

SCHUH: Naikan translates into introspection, and that's exactly what the method does. You see yourself through the eyes of other people and thus get a comprehensive image of yourself. This is the essence of Naikan: Really seeing yourself — in all nuances, shades, and facets. First and foremost I would say that Naikan is perception training, because my perception of myself and my environment becomes clearer and more conscious every day. This increases freedom because I do not experience myself as a victim of circumstances, but as an active part of my life. Because I can clearly acknowledge and recognize my past and my present, I can make peace with what was, and what is.

QUESTION: What fascinated you about Naikan so much that you wanted to continue with it?

SCHUH: The clarity, the warmth, the sustainability. In 1998 I titled my experiential report: On route to the light. I can still not express it any better. I saw everything through a type of fog before Naikan. The Naikan questions have clearly shown me what I have received, what I've done to others and what difficulties I have caused. It sounds corny, but it is the truth — I have found a lot of love again, learned to feel again. And I have recognized and learned that every person has their own way of expressing themselves. How do I as a selfish and arrogant being get to impose all my standards on others? And how weak I make myself by doing this, how many gestures and how much goodwill of my environment I don't perceive because of this. I could suddenly see that everything is right in front of me, I just need to look. The sun rose inside of me.

The experiences that I made in my first Naikan week changed my life. I didn't want to lose sight of the richness in my life, so I continued to practise Naikan. Some changes were difficult. And other things seemed to change as if by magic without my active involvement.

I always like to tell the story of the scissors. I am an orderly person and things have their place in my apartment, as do the scissors. If the scissors were not where they ought to be, the same routine followed: scissors not there, I was terribly annoyed, accused my partner of not having put them back, was sometimes annoyed for hours and even days. A few months after my first Naikan week the scissors were missing again. I looked for the scissors in the apartment quite calmly, didn't find them, stood in front of the drawer where they should actually have been. Suddenly, I stopped and thought: Something is very strange here... I was behaving very differently to how I otherwise would have — and without having planned it. That's when I thought: This Naikan is amazing...

QUESTION: What fascinates you about your work as a Naikan guide?

SCHUH: The variety of people that I get to know, and that such individual, trusting, undisguised encounters are possible in Naikan. And I always find it touching that such a simple method can make such a difference.

QUESTION: How do you see your role as a Naikan guide?

SCHUH: To me, every human being is like the ocean. I see the waves, the moving surface, the highlights and dramas of life, the traits, emotions, thoughts, stories. But every ocean is deep, the countless treasures are hidden there, the currents follow other laws, it is quieter and slower in a way. Everything is supported by the bottom of the sea — by the nature of the person, which affects everything. My perception is always on the depth, no matter how the surface is moving. I feel honoured and blessed when a person allows me insight into their depth and into their incomparable uniqueness.

My role is to respect every human being in all his facets and to appreciate these. And to never lose sight of that person's depth, even if he seems to be getting lost in the waves. If he starts to doubt himself, then I hope that my confidence can help him get through it.

QUESTION: Do you still practise Naikan yourself?

SCHUH: Yes, of course. I attend a Naikan retreat every three to four years, preferably for 10 days or longer. In everyday life I ask myself the three Naikan questions as warranted, if something is irritating me or if I want to find clarity in dealing with someone. I sometimes practise Naikan in the evening.

QUESTION: What do you want with regard to Naikan?

SCHUH: I want to guide Naikan until I breathe my last breath.

Contact

The author, Johanna Schuh, is the director of the Insightvoice Naikan Center in Vienna, and specializes in individual Naikan work. If you want to know more about her work or have any questions, please feel free to contact her:

Insightvoice Naikan Center Vienna
Rupertgasse 2
1140 Vienna
Austria

www.insightvoice.at

www.naikan.ws/english

CPSIA information can be obtained
at www.ICGtesting.com
Printed in the USA
BVHW040721031118
532093BV00004B/15/P